Hi John

Enjoy the read

Set's talk

All the best

M.G

Mark Schmitt

FROM

# MADISON AVENUE

TO

# RIKERS
# ISLAND

# FROM

## MADISON AVENUE

## TO

# RIKERS ISLAND

### The Making of a
### SOCIAL ENTREPRENEUR

## MARK L. GOLDSMITH

*Advantage*

Published by Advantage, Charleston, South Carolina.
Member of Advantage Media Group.

ADVANTAGE is a registered trademark, and the Advantage colophon is a trademark of Advantage Media Group, Inc.

Printed in the United States of America.

10 9 8 7 6 5 4 3 2 1

ISBN: 978-1-64225-310-8
LCCN: 2021918150

Cover and layout design by George Stevens.

This publication is designed to provide accurate and authoritative information in regard to the subject matter covered. It is sold with the understanding that the publisher is not engaged in rendering legal, accounting, or other professional services. If legal advice or other expert assistance is required, the services of a competent professional person should be sought.

Advantage Media Group is proud to be a part of the Tree Neutral® program. Tree Neutral offsets the number of trees consumed in the production and printing of this book by taking proactive steps such as planting trees in direct proportion to the number of trees used to print books. To learn more about Tree Neutral, please visit **www.treeneutral.com**.

Advantage Media Group is a publisher of business, self-improvement, and professional development books and online learning. We help entrepreneurs, business leaders, and professionals share their Stories, Passion, and Knowledge to help others Learn & Grow. Do you have a manuscript or book idea that you would like us to consider for publishing? Please visit **advantagefamily.com**.

*This book is dedicated
first and foremost to my wife,
Dr. Arlene Goldsmith,
who suggested that I go to
Principal for a Day (PFAD)
in the first place—then mentored
me in the world of social service
for over 17 years,
and to
Gloria Ortiz,
the principal of the Horizon Academy,
who urged me to keep returning to her
school on Rikers Island to meet with the guys
for over 15 years—which is what I did.*

# CONTENTS

# PREFACE

*Follow your passion, be prepared to work hard and sacrifice,
and above all, don't let anyone limit your dreams.*
**—DONOVAN BAILEY**

A significant number of US senior citizens are coming to the same decision I made when I decided to move from corporate America to the world of social services. While some senior citizens are facing retirement and others are simply looking for a new journey, many have a remarkable variety of skills that could greatly impact the nonprofit world. Combining those hard-earned skills with a passion to help cure a social ill can make a huge difference in the lives of people in need.

Even before the pandemic, several studies reflected the fact that older employees aren't being treated the same as their younger counterparts in the workplace. The assumption is that long-term employees have benefitted from their so-called experience premiums, and their collective years on the job have made them less likely to be terminated in economic downturns. However, the well-earned hierarchy of these employees has actually been diminished for quite some time, and the combination of a rising virtual economy, unenforced age-discrimination laws, and weakened unions have led to a further decline in a respected work environment for older people.

The combination of the coronavirus and the resulting recession has had a significant impact on future employment options in this country. Those combined factors have accelerated involuntary retirements at higher rates than in any previous decade. As is always the case, this situation has been worse for older men and women, Black and Latinx workers, and the uneducated.

**I believe that a mission backed by passion and enhanced by skills will almost always have a successful outcome.**

Most of those affected retirees have given little thought to what they might do once their time at a workplace comes to an end. While they may have vague notions about their plans, the majority of retirees do not recognize that their professional skills are transferable to the social service world and could greatly benefit others.

I personally moved from the corporate world to social entrepreneurship by transferring my years of experience and skills honed during my corporate years to the not-for-profit sector. My passion to help young men get out and stay out of the criminal justice system ended up being the secret sauce to my success, and I believe that a mission backed by passion and enhanced by skills will almost always have a successful outcome.

I hope that my story will motivate you to seriously take a look at volunteering in a social service agency. When I made the decision to shift my skills and passion, I not only helped create brand-new lives for my clients, but I also created a whole new life for myself. I feel privileged to be able to do the work that I now do, and it never feels like a job or a chore.

*Find a job you enjoy doing, and you will never have to work a day in your life.*
**—MARK TWAIN**

# ACKNOWLEDGMENTS

First and foremost, to my inner circle think tank who helped guide me from the inception of the writing of the book right up until it was "put to bed" and published:

Rick Smith, Andrew Serwer, and Andrew Konigsberg.

My daughter, Dr. Jennifer Adams; my son-in-law, Benjamin Adams; my son, Scott Goldsmith; and my daughter-in-law, Dr. Caitlin Fiss.

My sidekicks on the GOSO board of directors: Charles and Seryl Kushner, Richard and Freya Block, Ira and Karen Wachtel, Erich and Pam Linker, and Fred Pfaff, who have all been there for me from the get-go!

Chairman Reg Andre, Vice Chair Norm Merritt, John Berman, Brian Morrell, Jeremy Miller, Paul Netter, Jake Weinig, former board members Marvin Schechter, Steve Gutman and Julian Taub, and the entire board of directors of GOSO.

Dr. Jocelynn Rainey, Cal Mathis, Paul Gutkowski, John Atchison, and Tony Smith.

My brother Dr. Frank Goldsmith and his wife Barbara Storace. My brother-in-law Dr. Richard Levine and his wife Faith. My four granddaughters: Julia and Eleanor Adams and Aidan and Lucy Goldsmith.

The staff, and most importantly, the social workers of Getting Out and Staying Out.

The staff of Save East Harlem, headed up by Omar Jackson and Jayvon Alexander.

The Department of Education teachers of the GED program at GOSO—Priya Seshan.

The staffs of the Horizon and East River Academies on Rikers Island, especially the social workers and psychologists.

The corrections officers on Rikers Island.

John and Justine Leguizamo, Senator Corey Booker, Mariano Rivera and Wendy Neu.

Molly Foster Gribb, Dr. James Hutchison, and James Schry—my high school friends who have kept me grounded for over sixty-five years.

The New York Eight Pack: Dr. Richard and Ilene Dolins, Dr. Simon and Elaine Parisier, Drs. Sam and Linda Basch, and Arthur and Dianne Abbey. Barbara Rauch and in memory of Peter Rauch and Iris Abrons and in memory of Richard Abrons. David Pachter.

Bruce Rosenstein, Frances Hesselbein, Jonathan Knee, Sam Fremont Smith, Cheryl Kraemer, Julia Friedman, Elena Engel, and Robert and Julie de Luxembourg.

Assistant Commissioner Frances Torres of the New York City Department of Correction on Rikers Island.

The New York City Department of Education: Dr. Tim Lisante, Robert Zweig, Anthony Tassi, former Director Adult Education, and Bernard Gassaway.

The New York City Council.

The Mayor's Office of Criminal Justice—Eric Cumberbatch and Jessica Mofield.

All the foundations that generously supported GOSO.

Our supporters who attended our annual benefits.

Most importantly—all the close to 10,000 young men whom GOSO was honored to help by leveling the playing field for them to enable them to achieve jobs that led to careers and economic independence.

# INTRODUCTION

*It's not whether you get knocked down; it's whether you get up.*
**—VINCE LOMBARDI**

I grew up in Johnstown, Pennsylvania (famous for the flood of 1889). Before making the trek to Penn State University, I consumed too much alcohol at my going-away party, got behind the wheel of the family car, and ended up getting into an accident with a police car. I was arrested, booked, and locked up in the city jail. This life-changing incident occurred over sixty years ago, but I can still hear the clanging of the cell door closing behind me and feel the cold bench that I proceeded to lie down on before I passed out like it was yesterday.

After I came to, my only concern was how I was going to explain this to my parents. I made my one phone call and asked them to come down to the jail to release me. It was the most difficult phone call I have ever had to make. They paid my fine, and I was let go, and as to be expected, the ride home was agonizing. I kept apologizing, and they said, "Let's just move on, but you have really disappointed us."

My embarrassment spilled into the next day, when the Johnstown *Tribune-Democrat* reported on my biggest mistake. The headline said something along the lines of, "Meyer Goldsmith bailed out his son

Mark Goldsmith, who had been arrested the previous night for drunk driving."

Not only was I beyond embarrassed but I had zero excuses for my behavior.

I moved on from Penn State after two years and joined the United States Navy, where I initially fell in love with New York City. When our ship was docked in NYC for a weekend, my love of the city sprang to life, and I took in all the sights that lined the metropolis that would one day be my permanent home.

After I was honorably discharged from the navy, my main goal was to move to New York, and my father referred me to his company's office there, where I was hired as the assistant sales manager.

During the four years I worked at my father's company, I met my wife of sixty years, Dr. Arlene Levine, who was attending Columbia University's School of Social Work at the time. Telling her that I was going to be the guy who "made it" without a college education fell on deaf ears. She gave me the incentive to try night school, which is what I did full time at NYU, where I earned a BA in political science. During my senior year at NYU, I began searching for a sales and marketing job and applied to Pfizer, in their Coty Perfume division. They offered me a position earning twice as much as I had been earning at my father's company.

At Coty, I was given a budget and charged with organizing a sales meeting to launch a new fragrance. Following the meeting, I was promoted and informed that it was the best sales meeting the company had ever had. I began to recognize that I had entrepreneurial talent and energy, which I was not afraid to put into action given the opportunity.

At the same time, I enrolled in and was excelling in graduate school for my MBA degree, and I saw it as another notch in my belt to ensure that I would be the complete candidate for any level marketing position available.

Even though I was a corporate executive, my entrepreneurial spirit was also launched at that time. It was the single most important talent that I possessed, and I used it to propel me to the top of major corporations. Eventually, this passion and drive helped me launch my own company, as well as my own not-for-profit organization.

After two years at Coty, I was approached by Revlon, the industry leader at the time. I interviewed and was offered a position as marketing manager, responsible for their men's fragrances. Soon after that, Fabergé made me an offer to become their director of marketing of the Brut brand, the top men's fragrance brand in the country. While running Brut, I learned the importance of celebrity endorsements, as I worked closely with Muhammad Ali and Joe Namath.

I later ran Lanvin and Yves Saint Laurent, followed by the Japanese company Shiseido. Finally, I was the executive vice president of the Almay hypoallergenic brand for eight years before starting my own bartering and trading company, Inventory Management Systems (IMS), which delivered an important solution to major corporations' inventory problems. Initiating a start-up company gave me new, invaluable experiences that I was going to be able to call on when I started my not-for-profit organization, Getting Out and Staying Out (GOSO).

While working for a variety of different organizations, I gained experience in all facets of corporate America, including sales, marketing, finance, administration, human resources, and advertising. I began to consider that it might not be that difficult to transfer those skills to another arena.

As I started to think about retirement, I realized that I also had the talent needed to start an organization from scratch. I had launched many successful cosmetic brands as well as the IMS company. But at that point in time, it never occurred to me that the new organization Getting Out and Staying Out might be in the not-for-profit world. That was the last thing on my mind when my wife suggested that I volunteer for the Principal for a Day (PFAD) program in New York City, where volunteers go into the public school system one day a year and talk to teenagers about their future. I asked for the toughest school in New York City, and I got my wish.

Approximately sixty years after my going away party, I made it back to jail. This time around, there was no formidable sound of the jail cell door clicking into place as it locked me in. This time I was there for a very different reason. As part of the PFAD program, I had volunteered to talk with the toughest students in the city and gotten my wish by being assigned to Horizon Academy, run by the Department of Education (DOE) at the infamous Rikers Island jail in New York City.

# CHAPTER ONE

# My Very First Day on Rikers Island

*Every great dream begins with a dreamer. Always remember,
you have within you the strength, the patience, and the
passion to reach for the stars to change the world.*
**—HARRIET TUBMAN**

Rikers Island is a unique criminal justice facility which houses both men and women of all ages. People are there in various stages of the criminal justice system, including detainees with open cases awaiting trial, as well as those convicted of a misdemeanor, doing less that one year's time. Anyone convicted of a felony and sentenced to more than one year's time must do that time in an upstate New York prison. Since very few, if any, can post bail, the time that they spend on Rikers Island awaiting final adjudication of their cases can range from one month to a full year or more, in some complicated cases. In GOSO's entire history on Rikers Island, not a single young man who I had worked with bailed out. The bail system presently in place in NYC is long overdue for a major overhaul to ensure that people without means are able to be in the community while their cases are being adjudicated.

To reach Rikers Island from Manhattan, where I live, I had to use the Triborough Bridge to Queens and exit onto the Grand Central Parkway, past LaGuardia Airport, exiting approximately one mile past the airport. I parked my car on the Queens side of a small bridge leading to the actual jail and then boarded a small minibus, which takes visitors over the small bridge to the George Motchan Detention Center (GMDC), named after former warden George Motchan.

Once inside the building, I cleared security through the clanging doors and was asked to check any electronic equipment with the front desk. At no time during this process did I feel any trepidation. As a former corporate executive, I had been in tough spots before and had learned to develop a presence that let everyone around me know that I was a force to be reckoned with. In my suit and tie, I walked with authority, making it clear that I expected to be treated with respect. At the same time, I fully understood and respected the fact that the Department of Correction (DOC) was in total control. I was a guest in their house, and going forward, I let every Rikers Island visitor who accompanied me know that they were also guests in DOC's house. It was what enabled me and the program that I eventually established to be allowed access and be treated with respect.

As I sat waiting to go into the principal's office, my first thought was, "Well, here I go again." In high school when I got called into the principal's office, it was not because I was being honored or congratulated in any fashion. Simply said, they were not pleasant happenings in any way.

During this time, I had thoughts swirling around in my head about what I was going to say to the young men in my class. What could a former cosmetic industry executive possibly say to them to hold their interest? I was almost certain they wouldn't be very interested in lipstick and nail enamel. They might show interest in the bright light of the advertising world, and they certainly would be curious about the beautiful models I had worked with. What did I want to get out of the experience? Truthfully, I did not have a clue. I was there because my wife suggested that I should be a Principal for a Day because I was good with teenagers. Little did I know that I was going to get as much out of the experience as the young men would.

I was then led into Principal Gloria Ortiz's office. She was the one responsible for establishing the school approximately ten years prior to that day. In my briefing with Ms. Ortiz, she explained that the student body would not be that much different from any high school in New York City. However, since the students were over the age of sixteen, they were not mandated to come to school, and they were there voluntarily. She also mentioned that the majority of the men would be of color, and the statistics showed the breakdown as 50 percent Black, 35 percent Latinx, and only 15 percent White.

Ms. Ortiz indicated that for the most part they would be well behaved, even though there would be no security guard in the classroom. She believed that they would listen up, at least for a while, since it was a unique day at the school, and any bad behavior would not be tolerated.

Most of the young men had never experienced a PFAD program, and they would be inquisitive, at least at the very beginning of the presentation.

She wasn't wrong. From the moment I walked into the classroom, they were totally engaged because we were establishing some common ground. I was a Knicks fan and season ticket holder, and they all loved professional basketball. It also helped that I had been on a championship basketball team growing up in Pennsylvania, so I knew the details of the game as well as they did, if not better.

We had an extended conversation over the fact that when I played high school basketball in Pennsylvania, I played the role of the playmaker. We didn't have point guards and shooting guards like they have today in both college and professional basketball. Nearly every one of them said they played basketball, and most likely they were all much better than I ever was.

They were impressed by the fact that I was a Knicks season ticket holder and had watched famous idols of theirs like Michael Jordan, Magic Johnson, Kobe Bryant, Reggie Miller, and others beat up on the Knicks.

I think that I earned a few points with them because I was so knowledgeable about a sport that every one of them cared about. The three major sports in the US are baseball, football, and basketball, and the latter is dominated by men of color. The fact that a White businessman could "talk the talk" when it came to professional athletes that they admired was quite the eye-opener for them.

These students were also big fans of music, and they talked hip-hop while I talked rock and roll. They were surprised that I knew virtually all of the artists that we discussed in both segments even though the majority of the artists were of color. As a music buff, I couldn't care less whether the singers were Black or White.

They appreciated the fact that Otis Redding was my personal favorite, and they were shocked when they found out that I knew who Tupac Shakur was. The students' substance abuse centered primarily around marijuana as opposed to excessive beer drinking, which is what my high school days in the fifties were all about. We also discussed their potential business careers, and the ones that proved to be most interesting to the majority of them were business, sales, finance, and real estate.

The first thirty minutes of the class were spent getting to know one another by engaging in topics that were of interest to them. The difference between this visit and their everyday lives was that somebody was listening to them instead of forcing them to say or do something they had no interest in doing.

I had the distinct feeling that this might have been the first time these students had ever had a conversation with a White man in a suit and tie who wasn't a teacher, social worker, or a counselor of some sort. For the most part, they did not seem to be interested in education, but then again, neither was I in high school. They had their share of troublemakers in the school, something that I could easily relate to. I shared the instance when I was suspended from high school for paying a fellow student a bribe to kiss the beautiful, young music teacher. They thought that was very funny, but at this point in time, they did not have any interest in sharing their stories with me. We weren't quite there yet.

It didn't take long for them to share their opinions regarding how they felt about corrections officers and the NYC police. Needless to say, they were not very complimentary. However, I suggested that the vast majority of both groups, maybe 90 percent of them, were really OK and just doing their jobs, and only perhaps 10 percent were troublemakers, and they agreed with me. I followed this up, stating that most likely 90 percent of the students at Horizon Academy were not really bad guys, and 10 percent of them were never going to change their behavior and would probably keep coming back to Rikers Island after they were released. Again, they agreed. I think they appreciated my straight talking and felt comfortable responding in the same fashion.

I decided to center the main discussion for the day around an analogy between General Motors (GM) and a drug cartel. I gave them a brief outline of how GM was organized: management, sales, marketing, administration, finance, public relations, and advertising. I then asked them to give me a quick review on how much they knew about how the drug business worked organizationally.

I wanted to know, How did they get their supply of drugs to sell? What were the margins between what they paid for the drugs and what they sold them for? Was there a training period? Who did they report to other than themselves? How did they avoid getting arrested? Were they assigned territories to sell in? How did they get paid, by commission or salary?

For these guys, drugs were a way of life in the communities in which they grew up. They were either a user, seller, or an observer of the drug culture, and for many, drugs destroyed their families, and it was impossible to escape from the turmoil of drugs and addiction. So it wasn't shocking that drug-associated crimes made up a large part of their charges.

I then matched the two organizations on the blackboard and pointed out that the jobs that they had moving drugs were the same jobs that existed in corporate America. Some guys were good with numbers, both the numbers game and keeping the finances. I explained that there was an entire finance division at GM populated by experienced finance executives; however, there were also young administrative assistants doing the paperwork. The actual selling of the drugs on the street that they did was not unlike selling cars in a showroom. Selecting the right guys to be part of their sales network was parallel with GM's personnel department, which was responsible for hiring. They were truly amazed that their talents used in selling drugs on the street were comparable to the work done in the corporate world.

And, more importantly to them, they didn't realize that they could actually make more money in a corporation than they made selling drugs, without the threat of being arrested.

When I asked what industries were of interest to them, quite a few mentioned real estate. We then had an extended conversation about the real estate business and the many jobs that existed in that business: leasing, renting, sales, and management. Most were interested in sales.

We then ventured into the subject of employment and jobs and discussed the application process, including cover letters and resumes for a regular job and what it would take for them to become successful. They were shocked to hear that showing up on time or early, working really hard, taking the initiative to do extra work, and only being absent when truly necessary were the keys to my success and could be the answer to their success as well. Most importantly I focused on starting at the bottom and moving up, which is exactly how I made it in the corporate world.

At the end of the day, the corrections officers asked me what I did to keep the students' interest. They could not believe that they had listened so intently to me. I had a meeting with the principal, the corrections officers, and the warden, and we discussed what had transpired during my session with the guys. They were totally amazed that I was able to command their attention for the entire two hours I spent with them and literally could not believe it.

It was such a rewarding and satisfying day that I asked the principal if she would like me to come back after PFAD and continue to talk to the guys as a volunteer. She enthusiastically agreed. A White guy in the suit with a button-down shirt and tie had talked to them about what interested them. I had turned the conversation to a discussion about what they wanted to do with their lives once they had finished doing their time on Rikers Island. I believe that no one had ever asked them that question in their entire lives, and for once they felt a sense of hope and belonging. Their answers were phenomenal.

Sales primarily, but also stocks and bonds, a big interest in real estate, teaching, and coaching.

As I was leaving, a common phrase stood out in my mind: *There but for the grace of God goes any one of us.* I thought back to my night in jail in Johnstown, Pennsylvania, and the circumstances that had put me there. Had I been Black or Latinx, with no resources, including the ability to post bail, and that had happened to me in NYC, I would have ended up on Rikers Island just like the students that I had just talked to. Considering the amount of violence that takes place on Rikers Island and the amount of time that it takes to get a case finalized, there is no telling what might have happened to me.

**I had turned the conversation to a discussion about what they wanted to do with their lives once they had finished doing their time on Rikers Island. I believe that no one had ever asked them that question in their entire lives, and for once they felt a sense of hope and belonging.**

As I was driving home, I was really exhilarated. I felt that I had a done a really good job with the students, and I was confident that they had gotten something different and unanticipated out of the day. Personally, I felt that I had used my business and basketball skills with them in a way that it became as unique an experience for me as it had been for them.

When I returned home and related the day's experiences to my wife, she was not surprised that I'd had a rewarding day. Running a childcare agency in NYC, she had her own experiences regarding her clients' family members who had spent time in jail. It did not surprise her that I found the guys to be very bright and receptive to my suggestions regarding what they might do about their futures once released.

At the end of that first day, I made a decision to return to Rikers Island one day to meet with the guys again. It had been so profoundly rewarding, and the great satisfaction that it gave me made me believe I could make a difference in these young men's lives.

Maybe Rikers Island wasn't the end of the world for them. Just maybe there was a world out there where they might achieve success in a way that put money in their pockets and enabled them to have a life free from the criminal justice system.

What was most important to me was that I was able to deliver my message in a way that caused them to pay attention for several hours. I had been up for the challenge of engaging them, keeping their interest, and not being just another Principal for a Day. However, the most surprising thing of all was discovering how much I got out of the day and how I felt compelled to make a difference in their lives going forward.

# CHAPTER TWO

# From Rikers Island to Starbucks

*Nothing great in the world has ever been accomplished without passion.*
**—GEORG WILHELM FRIEDRICH HEGEL**

A s it turned out, for a myriad of reasons, I did not return to Rikers Island for an entire year. Getting back into the jail to meet with the guys on my own was easier said than done. There was significant red tape, and I was not part of any program, nor did I want to be. Several other factors played a role in my delay in getting back there. My consulting business was rapidly growing, making time an issue, and the added difficulty of having to be part of a program that I would need to interview with proved to be a bridge too far; no pun intended.

Before I knew it, it was time for the annual Principal for a Day event again, and I immediately had a plan in place. I went down to register and requested to be sent back to Rikers Island. Before I could finish my request, they informed me that a request had already been made for my placement. The principal of Horizon Academy on Rikers Island, Gloria Ortiz, had asked that I be assigned to her school again. Little did they know, that was exactly where I wanted to go.

On that first trip back to Rikers Island, I brought books to distribute to the guys and started conversations with them regarding job opportunities that they might pursue once they were released. Out of all the questions I received from the guys on that first day back, one stood out among the rest. When I handed this particular gentleman a book, he asked me if it was his to keep. I said, "Of course," and he remarked that it was the first time that anyone had ever given him a book that was his to keep. It was quite shocking to me that this nineteen-year-old young man had never been given a book to keep.

For the balance of that first year, I continued to return to Rikers Island, visiting each of the individual jails that housed the eighteen- to twenty-four-year-old young men. GMDC, GRVC, AMKC, OBCC, and the infirmary housed in NIC are the facilities where I spent the majority of my time with the guys. Each of these facilities held a bit of history. The GMDC was originally opened as a correctional institution for females in 1971 before the 1988 opening of the Rose M. Singer Center for Women. When it was reopened as a male detention center, it was named after George Motchan, a seventeen-year veteran corrections officer who was shot in the line of duty. It is now being used as a training academy annex and wellness center for DOC staff.

The George R. Vierno Center (GRVC) was named after a former chief of department and acting commissioner. Originally opened in 1991, GRVC was expanded in 1993 and houses detained and sentenced male adults.

As the largest facility on Rikers Island, the Anna M. Kross Center (AMKC) was named after the DOC's second female commissioner, and its forty acres of property are home to a methadone detoxification unit. It also houses detained and sentenced male adults.

The North Infirmary Command (NIC) is made up of two buildings, one of which was the original Rikers Island Hospital built in 1932. While it houses detainees with acute medical conditions and those with disabilities, it is also home to some general population detainees.

Each of the five different facilities required special clearances, which was a necessary challenge that I had to face, and I managed to obtain the clearances in one day. Not an easy feat.

The charges against the young men ranged from misdemeanors to nonviolent and violent felonies, and it didn't take me long to realize that there was a very thin line between violent and nonviolent crimes. The difference in charges could be based on something as simple as the quantity of drugs they were accused of selling. I did not get heavily involved in their cases; however, I did write letters of support for them, and in special situations, I went to court on their behalf, which often led them to getting lesser sentences. Part of this unique process involved me working with their lawyers, which ultimately attracted many more participants to the program, causing it to grow at a steady pace.

Approximately six months after I started going to Rikers Island, thanks to my efforts in court on his behalf, a young man named John was offered an inpatient rehabilitation program in the city and was set to be released the following week. When we discussed what his plans might be once he was back home, I grew upset when I learned that he really didn't have a plan. His intention was to go back to the "same old, same old," a life that could very well lead to another arrest and more time at Rikers Island. It was a meaningless circle that he couldn't seem to get past.

I asked John if he would like to continue our conversations once he was released, and he was very enthusiastic about that possibility. Determining where to have those meetings was my next challenge. As a trial run, we set up an appointment to meet at the Starbucks at 39th Street and Madison Avenue. It turned out to be the perfect selection in that it had a men's room as well as inside and outside tables with some privacy.

I became one of their most well-known, frequent customers, as I drank more café lattes during that first year than any other customer. As an added bonus, my guys started to feel at home there, which was very important to me. Feeling safe and welcomed in a public facility in Midtown Manhattan was a new experience for most of the young men that I was working with. I continued working out of Starbucks for the first year of my new endeavor.

I am still in regular contact with John, since he is a member of the GOSO Coaching Club that I organized during my retirement. One of the most rewarding aspects of becoming a mentor, father figure, and now a grandfather figure in the lives of GOSO guys is the many letters I receive. I often get correspondence from these men passionately describing what it has meant to them to have an ongoing relationship with me and the GOSO organization, and how it has inspired them to dramatically alter the direction of their lives. For the most part, their lives have been characterized by ongoing disappointment from father figures, which is why receiving these grateful letters constantly reminds me of and energizes my decision to serve this community sixteen years ago.

My relationship with these young men has been pivotal in the creation of this book, which is why I decided to include some of their letters. The letters come from a blend of different young men, all of whom have been incarcerated at one time or another over the last twelve years. Some are still incarcerated, but most of them are out after doing both long- and short-term periods of time in both Rikers Island as well as upstate prisons.

Starbucks became my very first unofficial office in Manhattan and, most importantly, it was rent free. That was where I would meet the guys to discuss how they were doing since they'd been released. We discussed their enrolling in General Educational Development (GED) programs and community colleges, as well as working on their resumes and cover letters.

Our conversations at Starbucks became much more relaxed than they had been on Rikers Island, and the guys were more willing to open up to me and share aspects of their lives.

It was at that time that I began to consider starting an official not-for-profit reentry program in NYC for young men eighteen to twenty-four years of age. I felt I was making a real difference in the guys' lives, and that rewarding feeling propelled me to start brainstorming ideas for what my nonprofit would entail.

I did not have a clear idea about what this new agency might look like. All I knew was that I was having a profound effect on the guys that I was working with. They were getting jobs, going back to school, and not going back to the behavior that had caused them to be sent to Rikers Island in the first place. I often found myself questioning why and how this was all coming to fruition.

After a lot of deep thought, I realized that it was simply because they trusted me and

**Over time I had learned that these young men do not trust very many people, and they were coming to understand that their trust in our relationship was having a positive effect on their outcomes.**

believed that I had their best interests at heart. Over time I had learned that these young men did not trust very many people, and they were coming to understand that their trust in our relationship was having a positive effect on their outcomes in both education and the workplace.

The principal on Rikers Island had once mentioned that the young men I was meeting with had, for the most part, been terribly disappointed with their lives. It started with their family members who were absent due to their own problems. What made all the difference in their relationship with me was that I was there for them when they needed me, and I was consistent, executing and committing to all of my promises.

It was amazing that this whole process was taking place inside Rikers Island as well as at Starbucks, certainly two settings that were not ideal for in-depth conversations that involved the future of these young men's lives.

If I was going to continue doing this work, I needed to find a small office so that I could have a presence in the community and a proper space where I could meet the young men in privacy.

At this juncture, I must emphasize the importance of passion for one's mission. To start an organization, a social entrepreneur must first discover a need for that organization in society and then use creativity in every move to help resolve that need. When trying to determine if this is an endeavor that you want to undertake, you must first determine if you are indeed passionate about your mission, as passion is the number one ingredient in any endeavor.

You can only accomplish this by immersing yourself in your chosen endeavor, and most importantly, you must believe that you can make a significant, positive difference in the lives of your clients.

There are several ways to get involved in a not-for-profit organization, including volunteer work, fundraising, becoming a board member, or helping with an annual benefit. If after doing one or more of these activities, you determine that you can make that difference, it is time to get started. If you cannot, it might be time to either find another cause to pursue or perhaps to find another opportunity in the for-profit sector of our economy.

There was no question that I had found my calling in working with young men eighteen to twenty-four years of age involved in the criminal justice system: because as I had mentioned before, "There but for the grace of God goes any one of us." I knew that I could've easily been in the same position as the majority of the men I was helping. Instead, because I had a caring father who bailed me out of a situation that would have ruined my life had I been of color in New York City, I felt that I was in a perfect position to help young men like I once was to ensure their lives were not ruined by making one stupid mistake as a teenager, as I had done.

# CHAPTER THREE

# Making a Profit or Making a Difference

*Do not go where the path may lead; go instead*
*where there is no path, and leave a trail.*
**—WINSTON CHURCHILL**

Approximately ten years ago, there was a series on television called *Mad Men*. It was the story of executives in the advertising business, which matched the world I lived in for over twenty-five years.

When I was discharged from the Navy, I found a job in New York City's garment district, and that was how I made it from Johnstown, Pennsylvania to New York City. While there, I was hired by Pfizer in their Coty division while pursuing my master's degree at night at NYU. I then transitioned to Revlon, where I led their men's fragrance division before making the move to manage marketing for Brut cologne. During my time at Brut, I had the opportunity to meet several celebrities who we used as spokesmen for the brand. I mention that here to accentuate how using for-profit experiences helped me to build Getting Out and Staying Out. I learned how to network and get my brand in front of the consumer, just as I later used celebrities to volunteer and raise awareness for GOSO. I will segue into those experiences later in the book.

While in the advertising business, I worked with Muhammed Ali, who I had to convince to be part of an ad created by our agency instead of an ad that he suggested that went like this:

Ali: "Honey, bring my Brut." No response. "Honey, bring me my Brut." After no response, he yelled it again, and this time here comes his wife, dragging that mean, old Sonny Liston into his bathroom, at which time he says, "I don't want that ugly old brute; I want my Brut from Fabergé."

We had a good laugh, and he agreed to go with the agency's suggestion. I will never forget the size of his hand when we shook hands goodbye as he left my office. No wonder he packed such a wallop!

Another celebrity I had a chance to meet at a party was Joe Namath, chatting with Howard Cosell. We spoke about western Pennsylvania high school football at length, since we both grew up in western Pennsylvania. He was amazed that a guy at a cocktail party in NYC knew about his high school football team. Once again, just as Namath was paid to support my Brut brand, we at GOSO needed to convince high-profile people to talk positively about GOSO. It all came full circle, and my experience in the for-profit world spilled into my not-for-profit world.

Later in my career, having run Yves Saint Laurent's fragrance division, I had to deal with Yves in all aspects of the brands. I learned that he loved the color black, and that enabled me to get quick decisions, which is another perfect example of how I dealt with high-profile people to get my job done well.

Later in my career, I was responsible for communicating with regulatory agencies in Washington, DC, when I ran a hypoallergenic brand called Almay that needed FDA approval for the use of the terminology. I networked with Leonard Lauder. We went to DC to explain the procedures that allowed us to use the terms "hypoallergenic" and "allergy tested." This came in handy when I later networked with other reentry organizations, city officials, and the White House on criminal justice reform. (Details on that initiative later.)

Once again, when it came time for me to appeal to New York City and New York State for funding for GOSO, I was able to use my for-profit experience to convince them to approve my formal requests for funding that eventually took GOSO to a $5 million budget, starting from scratch in a highly competitive funding market. Those early years were particularly tough financially, so much so that I once had to ask my wife if we could help GOSO make a payroll, which she agreed to do, and then of course, we were reimbursed once the funds became available.

There are over twelve million people, 10 percent of all workers, employed in the nonprofit world, and there are probably well over one million not-for-profit organizations and close to one hundred million volunteers. These numbers equate to a lot of opportunity. Should you decide that there was a cause that you were interested in and felt that you could make a difference, just give an agency a call and volunteer.

With the pandemic now well into its second year, there are significant social service needs that are serious and require solutions on an urgent basis.

Structural racism has contributed to large segments of our society being left behind, which has led to a larger portion of people of color dying from the virus. With schools being closed, children in poor communities have faced more setbacks than children in more prosperous segments of our society. Groups that fall under the low-income category need help, and they need it now.

At the same time, there are hundreds of thousands of employees who have been laid off and will never be rehired at their old positions because the company that they formerly worked for no longer has a need for their services.

**Structural racism has led to large segments of our society being left behind in the vaccination process, which means that a larger portion of people of color have died from the virus.**

The not-for-profit world could be a logical move for individuals who have a strong social conscience and a desire to do something about a particular issue. They also may or may not have reached the height of their professional possibilities due to their advanced age and lack of technical training. While this may cause many employees great frustration and make them think they have limited options, those with energy and a desire to make a difference can combine their experience with passion and find work in a not-for-profit.

When I still had one foot in the for-profit world, I had some homework to do if I was going to make the move into the not-for-profit world. I needed to understand the difference between a for-profit and a not-for-profit, and from that point, I had to determine if my skills could make the shift.

My wife had spent her entire career in not-for-profits, so I spent a great deal of time talking to her about the differences in the all-important decision-making process between a for-profit and not-for-profit. It turned out that decision-making and procedural processes were the single most different aspect of all.

In the corporate world, I jokingly referred to myself as a benevolent despot. I had a reputation of being a well-respected leader, and I made it a priority to teach my employees as much as I managed them, making sure that their time with me was well spent. Furthermore, I always met with people who reported to me; however, in the end I probably made too many decisions on my own. In the entrepreneurial world, it was not uncommon for that to be the case. When I made the transition to the not-for-profit world, I quickly realized that my style of management would have to change, and instead of being the sole decision maker, I was now working with a team to make important decisions.

The issue at hand:

Economist Milton Friedman said it best:

"The primary purpose of a business organization is to *make a profit*."

If that is the case—what is the purpose of a social service organization? The primary purpose of a social organization is to make a difference in the lives of others, whether that is through direct service or by creating changes in the rules and regulations of our society and government. And the end result is always a positive effect on others.

Like the many social entrepreneurs who paved the path before me, I was at a crossroads. In addition to the two days a week I was spending with the guys from Rikers Island, I was also responsible for running my highly profitable barter business called Inventory Management Systems (IMS). We worked with major corporations facilitating their exchange of excess inventories for media, relieving them of having to take huge financial losses. Simply said, my plate was full.

I had to make a decision, and I believe that the decision was made for me by the satisfaction I was feeling from working with the young men in the Rikers Island jail in NYC and in Starbucks, once they were released. The feeling that I was making a profound difference in their lives was reflected in the decisions these men were making.

Many whom I mentored were getting out and staying out of Rikers Island simply because they were finding jobs and achieving a life they had never imagined. They were changing their own paths because they were bolstered by my confidence in them, and that feeling of reward was impossible to let go of.

My business, while thriving, was not giving me anywhere near the satisfaction that I was getting from working with the young men, the age of which was then expanded to include sixteen- and seventeen-year-olds. As a young man I had floundered, not as badly as the guys with whom I was working, but I had not excelled at their age, and I had all of the benefits derived from a middle-class family. It was no wonder these men ended up in the criminal justice system, when most of them grew up in poverty, needed public assistance, entered the foster care system, were lost in extremely crowded schools, and came face-to-face with addiction.

When I put my cards on the table, it was no contest. I closed my business and went full speed ahead with my focus fueled by the feel-good emotions that came along with helping others. I was determined to become a social entrepreneur working in the criminal justice system with young men sixteen to twenty-four years of age.

One of the first things I tackled when I put my foot on the gas to be a social entrepreneur was navigating my way through the funding process of not-for-profits.

As you can imagine, there are as many differences as there are similarities in the not-for-profit and for-profit worlds. Funding is one of those major differences, and for good reason.

A business organization raises funds by borrowing from a financial institution or private investors based on a business plan that produces a profit while providing a payback plan to the investor. A not-for-profit, on the other hand, raises funds by promising to make a difference in the lives of those who fall under a specific population. They do this by using donations from private sources, governments (city, state, and federal), and foundations. The payback plan takes the form of performance reviews that specifically outline how the not-for-profit used specific funding to produce the promised results that they had requested in their grant proposal.

This is an area that GOSO excelled in. We prided ourselves in not just meeting our projected outcomes but exceeding them. It is also an area that utilized my corporate background to a great extent, since I had spent thirty-five years reporting on activities and forecasting results in corporations as well as my privately held company.

My next priority was to acquire an office where I could have a presence in the community and a proper space to meet the GOSO members. I wanted to prioritize convenience for the young men, which was why I opted to set up shop in East Harlem, next door to Harlem, where many of them came from, and the closest point in Manhattan to Rikers Island.

After I determined the space where all the action would take place, it was time to establish a name for the agency. In any new endeavor, I feel that it is important that the name of the entity reflect the goals of the organization. The mission of my not-for-profit would be assisting young men, now expanding to sixteen to twenty-four years of age, to get out and stay out of the criminal justice system. I wanted to describe that process simply so when people saw it, it immediately made sense to them. And this was when Getting Out and Staying Out (GOSO) clicked into place.

During this time, it was crucial that I create a mission statement so I could articulate in just a few words exactly what the agency's focus would be.

Putting together a board of directors was also high on my to-do list. I had some specific people in mind who had indicated an interest in what I had been doing over the past year.

Staffing, on the other hand, was not high on my priority list at this point, because I had intended to be a one-man show with the help of an office assistant until I was able to raise funds. Up until this point, I had only used personal funds for the agency.

I did know that I would be hiring only master-level social workers to do the day-to-day work with the guys. This was at my wife's insistence, since her experience had taught her that in order to handle the emotional end of the agency's three pillars, with education and employment being the other two, I needed to have experienced social workers who could deal with the trauma experienced by the formerly incarcerated. Many of their emotions were compounded by structural racism, foster care, poverty, substance abuse, and homelessness.

I saw the way the Rikers Island social workers and psychologists worked with the guys, gaining their confidence when they were going through very difficult times in their lives. I needed to provide that same type of support once they were released into the communities they grew up in, where all of their problems started.

When it came to staffing, I knew that I had to hire or groom strong employees who could assist me in the management process and follow the agency's mission to consistently put clients first. The motto of GOSO is "It's all about the guys," which I follow thoroughly along with the entire staff and board of directors.

In the not-for-profit arena, an executive director is faced with the constant challenge of balancing staff salaries, which is every agency's biggest expense and vital to the programming. While I had much on my plate, my passion for the mission propelled me and helped me face the challenge head-on.

Further, before making my final decision, as I explored the not-for-profit world, I started to realize that I have always been a compassionate person and always one to root for the underdog. While I had spent the majority of my life immersed in my career, making changes and moving up the financial ladder, I maintained compassion for those who were less fortunate than me.

Every three or four years, I moved to a new company to continue my growth in both leadership and pay. When I reached the very top of the last companies I worked for, I resigned and formed my own corporation, which turned out to be my most successful venture of all. Being the sole decision maker of my own corporation suited my personality best, and it was a role that I had to transition out of for the not-for-profit that I was building. There was no way that my former management style was going to survive in the nonprofit world, even if I was going to be the founder, president, and CEO.

Finally and most importantly, the positive differences that I was helping to make in the lives of young men would far surpass, in my mind, the profit goals that I had worked to achieve for the first thirty-five years of my life in the corporate world.

# CHAPTER FOUR

# Name the Agency, the Mission Statement, Becoming a 501(c)(3)

*Leaders become great not because of their power, but because of their ability to empower others.*
**—JOHN MAXWELL**

I have always been a firm believer that the name of an organization should reflect exactly what the entity's business entails. By describing the mission of the organization in the actual name of the agency, you can kill two birds with one stone and paint a clear picture of your operation.

As I considered starting a not-for-profit in the criminal justice system, I kept coming back to the recidivism issue. Unfortunately, the vast majority of the young men did not beat their cases. Instead, they were convicted and kept on Rikers Island for a year or less to do misdemeanor time or sent to upstate prisons ("up top") to do felony time, both violent and nonviolent.

If I could make a dent in the absurd 65 percent recidivism rate for young men, both on Rikers Island and throughout the country, I would be making a real difference in our society, particularly in the Black and Latinx communities.

Since the young men's starting point would be inside the Rikers Island jail, the first objective would be for them to get out of Rikers Island by trying to attain justice. Once released, the object would be to assist them to not recidivate and get them on a path that would keep them out of the criminal justice system altogether. Based on the rate of relapse, there was a 65 percent chance they would be returning to Rikers Island at some point in time. They would then be placed on parole or probation, which was dependent on the location they were released from, and in many cases, they would violate the terms and be reincarcerated.

Knowing these facts, I was able to prioritize the not-for-profit's mission, and the most important aspect of the program would be for us to be there for them from the moment they were released. By taking advantage of our reentry program, they were going to be given a fantastic opportunity to stay out of jail, because they would be creating new lives for themselves through education and employment while gaining emotional stability.

Our main objective for these men was to get out and stay out of the criminal justice system after they either beat their case or spent time in a jail or prison before being released.

While running in Central Park one day, a light bulb went off in my head. The not-for-profit could be expressed in a simple thought that encapsulated the entire mission, and the name would be Getting Out and Staying Out (GOSO).

When you use that terminology in our society, most people understand that you are talking about the criminal justice system and getting out of a prison or jail. The key words, of course, were "staying out." Getting out was eventually going to happen based on the seriousness of the crime for which they had been convicted. Staying out was another matter, since they would be returning to the same communities that they'd come from, the same police precincts, the same conditions of life that plague the inner cities of our country.

## THE MISSION STATEMENT

The mission statement has evolved over fifteen years, starting out as a short statement focused on recidivism to one that is more focused on desired results and how to achieve them. As long as we did not veer too sharply from the original statement, I did not have an issue updating it to reflect change over the years.

## THE ORIGINAL MISSION STATEMENT

Getting Out and Staying Out is dedicated to drastically reducing the recidivism rate for eighteen- to twenty-four-year-old young men by ensuring economic independence through purposeful education and directed employment.

## THE UPDATED VERSION

The rationale for updating the mission statement was driven by the fact that many funding sources appreciated being told up-front how the lofty projected reduction from 65 percent to under 15 percent in recidivism was going to be achieved, rather than having to read through an entire request for funding to determine that. It is for this reason that we reworked the statement to include the following:

Getting Out and Staying Out (GOSO) empowers young men to avoid involvement in the criminal justice system by reshaping their futures through educational achievement, meaningful employment, and financial independence.

GOSO focuses on the individuals' capabilities and strengths as well as developmental needs and emotional well-being. Our aim is to promote personal, professional, and intellectual growth through goal-oriented programming and comprehensive social support services.

While I thought it would be important to try and stick to the original statement, necessity took precedence over that thinking. I used that approach on virtually every decision that I made for GOSO, from its inception date to the day I retired. I never stood on ceremony, as they say.

Being a highly competitive person, I did not want my funding competitors to have any advantage over GOSO.

The mission statement was the precise description and factual representation of the organization that potential funders or participants would see, whether it be on our website, in our written proposals, or part of any public or private conversations. It was the face of our organization and quickly became the most important document we would work with.

Most importantly, there would be a clearly stated return on their investment (ROI), should they decide to either join GOSO as a client or to fund this vital new reentry program.

## INCORPORATING AS A 501(C)(3)

Years ago, this process would have required hiring a law firm, spending countless hours and dollars; however, today the only requirement is the application for your state's tax status, all of which can be done online.

There are twenty different types of nonprofits under the Internal Revenue Code. Since the 501(c)(3) is the largest segment that deals with social issues, it was a given that I would select it for Getting Out and Staying Out.

## LEGAL ZOOM SERVICES WEBSITE

Simply follow their instructions, and you will see that the entire process of establishing a 501(c)(3) takes very little time. You must do your research to ensure there will be no naming conflicts with other not-for-profits, and the official paperwork should arrive back from your state within thirty days.

# CHAPTER FIVE

# It's All about the Guys

*You have to learn the rules of the game, and then*
*you have to play better than anyone else.*
**—ALBERT EINSTEIN**

After formalizing GOSO as a legal entity, I was determined to ensure the program was unique in every aspect of our work. I wanted to ensure that the GOSO program stood out from any other reentry organization, and I was unaware of any other program that had the lofty outcomes that I wanted to achieve.

I wanted the young men, the Department of Education, and the Department of Correction to know that GOSO was going to be a program where potential participants had to do something other than just sign up to become part of it. Further, we made it clear that our philosophy required real interest before GOSO would commit to the guys after they were released.

Therefore, a decision was made right from the get-go that there would be an admission process. This would be centered around an essay where the applicant spoke of their hopes and aspirations following their release from jail. We also required they provide us with their lawyer's names and telephone numbers.

There is a concept in business referred to as "skin in the game." It is a term made popular by Warren Buffett describing a situation where high-ranking insiders use their own money to buy stock in their own company, making them even more motivated to succeed. I used this analogy with the guys, forcing them to submit a request to join GOSO to prove that they were really interested as opposed to just showing up to hear me speak to them about job opportunities. I believe that all not-for-profits should do something similar when signing applicants up for their services to ensure that they know, from the get-go, that they had to do their part to make their participation in the program work. Simply said, it was not going to be a free ride.

At this point in time, they were not asked what their charges were, and that would come in our first face-to-face meeting. I wanted them to be focused solely on their futures, not on their pasts.

Many were reluctant to write the essay, so persistence was required. Once they learned that I was serious and would refuse to see them unless they wrote the letter, virtually every potential candidate wrote the essay.

The letters gave me a good idea of who they were, their level of English, grade achievement in high school, and potential for achieving their high school diploma or GED credentials, a two- or four-year college degree, or a certificate from a technical school.

It was important to establish the fact that their involvement with GOSO did not end on Rikers Island. If they were to beat their cases, GOSO would be waiting to assist them on the outside to further their careers and education and ensure that their emotional well-being was being attended to.

If they were obviously going to lose their case, they were advised by their counsel to take the best possible plea offered. We were very instrumental in getting them reduced pleas based on their remaining in our reentry program once they were eventually released. GOSO would be corresponding with them while they were incarcerated on Rikers Island or in a New York upstate prison until they were released, at which time they would come to our office in Harlem for counseling and mentoring. Part of this process also included the enrollment in the job readiness curriculum.

The upstate New York Prison Correspondence Program became an integral segment of GOSO, and it continues to this day. In addition to making visits upstate, I personally continue to correspond with young men whom I met over fifteen years ago. Several of those letters are included in the book. I highly recommend you read these letters, and you will learn how the guys blossomed.

One unique aspect of the program that evolved was that young men who had already left Rikers before I got there and were spending time in upstate prisons found out about us from fellow cellmates who had joined GOSO during their time on Rikers Island. They wrote to me, and I enrolled them in GOSO's correspondence program with the same benefits.

The guys took my suggestion that they take advantage of any and all educational and training programs that were offered in the facility where they were located. Several received high school and college degrees while incarcerated. Further, equally important to them was that in spite of the fact they were hundreds of miles away, GOSO had not forgotten about them. We were very interested in how they were functioning and coping with the fact that the same gangs they were associated with in the city still existed inside the prisons and could be dangerous to their health and welfare.

Finally, the fact that our personal relationship, having been so important to them while they were in the Rikers Island jail, was never going to disappear, and they grew confident that we would build on it over the years.

Why did I originally insist on the letter to get into the program? Because they needed to get used to being responsible for their individual destiny. I wanted them to do something about their future and then see the results of their actions. That practice has been continued right up to the present day.

> **Why did I originally insist on the letter to get into the program? Because they needed to get used to being responsible for their individual destiny.**

Having practical solutions to everyday problems in the workplace, once they were released, was also a key ingredient. For the most part, they did not have many friends or family members to give them that support.

As an example, a GOSO guy was working for an employer whose president was on the GOSO board of directors, and he was having trouble getting a raise. I was asked by his social worker to intervene, and I told her that I wanted to speak to the guy first. When I asked him if he had followed the procedure of requesting feedback from his superior before he brought up a raise, he said that he hadn't. He is now waiting for the right time to take that approach, and my guess is that he will be successful.

I had also taken the time to assess again exactly who the participants in the program were going to be. Who were these guys? How did they get to Rikers Island in the first place?

Assistance in this analysis came from a secret ingredient … my wife of nearly sixty years, Dr. Arlene Goldsmith. She had gone to Brandeis University for her undergraduate degree before obtaining her master's degree at Columbia University and her PhD in social work at Fordham University.

Arlene and I had been active in the Civil Rights Movement in the late fifties and early sixties, and Black lives have always mattered to both of us. She was the one that had marched with me in Harlem when the three young men were murdered in Mississippi. Later in our marriage, we worked together in Queens to help Black couples rent advertised apartments. If denied, the National Urban League stepped in and ensured they got the apartment. Most importantly, Arlene is the person who suggested that I be a Principal for a Day in the first place, and while she was not overjoyed that I was being sent to Rikers Island, she learned to live with it.

Following a twenty-year career as a social worker, Arlene founded New Alternatives for Children (NAC) in 1982, an agency that provides real help and real hope to thousands of children with disabilities and chronic illnesses and their families throughout New York City. Starting with half a desk, she grew NAC into a 30 MM agency with over 450 employees. With a successful foster care unit, she had been dealing with families of color in NYC and knew exactly who the young men were on Rikers Island, so she provided much guidance along the way.

It has been said that foster care is one of the pipelines to prison. A large percentage of the young men in GOSO had not finished high school. The majority of the population came from families living in poverty, where fathers were generally not present. Most had experienced severe trauma in their young lives and were raised by their grandmothers and aunts in kinship care instead of their birth mothers.

Homelessness would not be uncommon. Drugs were a major part of their lives, and gang membership was common. For the most part, society would have given up on these individuals, and they in turn had given up on themselves. These facts gave me an understanding of who the guys were who would be joining GOSO.

During my first few months at Rikers, I learned how willing the young men were to talk to me. It was a unique situation for them, talking to a White man about how they might make money legitimately rather than selling drugs or by being part of criminal gang involvement. Making money was very important to them, as they had grown up in poverty, in terrible neighborhoods on public assistance, without all of the glamour and niceties that they saw on television as well as in the movies if they could ever afford to go.

My being able to talk basketball did not hurt, either, as it was the sport they loved to play and watch. I was able to "talk the talk" about a topic they loved.

In prepandemic days, the sessions started with a firm handshake, not a fist bump, whether they liked it or not. They were strongly encouraged to get used to a professional handshake, as it is a sign of professionalism.

After reviewing their application letter with them, I then had a conversation about their case. When asked who was representing them, they told me they were being represented primarily by legal aides at no cost, or 18B lawyers (who practiced privately as well as on Rikers), and very few fully private lawyers whose cost they could not afford.

When I informed them that I would consider appearing in court on their behalf, should the need arise, they would respond with shock and appreciation.

Their charges ranged from misdemeanors to both violent and nonviolent felonies. Many of the guys were making their second or third trip back to Rikers Island after having been released and rearrested on new charges. We never spent a lot of time discussing their legal charges, as they could only be resolved in the courtroom.

For the most part, virtually every young man who joined GOSO was eventually going to be judged as guilty. Determining the best possible plea bargain that could be achieved by them was the only remaining question.

That was where GOSO came into the picture by providing letters of support and appearing in court on their behalf. These letters of support were backed up by the participant's application letter to GOSO, and the combination made a powerful statement that resulted in more lenient sentences for first timers.

Unfortunately, most of the guys in the program were convicted or took pleas that landed them in a New York State prison in upstate New York. Upstate prisons were always referred to as being "up top." Those stays could range anywhere from two years to life. Fortunately, many upstate facilities offered college by mail, and in my correspondence with the Rikers Island guys, I encouraged them to take advantage of the opportunity for college courses, urging them to earn degrees while they were incarcerated.

One of those guys who I met on Rikers Island in 2005 graduated as valedictorian from the alternative high school on Rikers Island. He eventually pleaded guilty and received a ten-year sentence. While up top, he earned a bachelor's degree from Ohio State, and he is now getting an MBA from Rutgers. The young man, named Anton, shared the following quote with me:

> Along the way, I created and built a business sending better-quality foods into the prisons of New York State. The company achieved $1 million in sales this year. Most importantly, I am finally off parole. You played a huge part in my life, and I hope you know I owe a lot of where I am today because of you. Keep changing lives, man; I hope one day I can do the same.

Once word got out that GOSO was an agency that became involved in their cases and they could attend voluntarily on Rikers Island at Horizon Academy, several more guys grew interested in speaking with me. At the same time, this gave me the opportunity to engage them in conversation that focused on both education as well as future employment once they were released. I believe that attendance also improved because of my presence in the school. At this point, GOSO was growing with promising young men who were dedicated to changing their lives.

One of those young men was Maliki, who took my entrepreneurial skills lecture seriously. When he was released, he started his own hauling company that recently won a contract to move GOSO into its new offices. His letter is included in the Appendix.

While I was well equipped to teach them about job skills and education, I did not have the skill set to deal with any trauma they might be experiencing, from either their time in jail or their life before they were incarcerated.

This realization led me to adopt another pillar of the agency, and I made the decision to include the three *E*'s as an essential part of the program: Education, Employment, and Emotional Well-Being. The addition of emotional well-being required that I only hire licensed MSW professionals who could deliver strength-based therapeutic intervention therapy that would lead to major, positive changes in the guys' mental health outcomes.

Discussions on their families, girlfriends, children, mothers, and grandmothers came up quite often; however, there was very little talk about the fathers of these men, which was very upsetting to me. Little did I know I would soon become a father or grandfather figure to them. To this day, I still get calls on Father's Day from guys who I have known for more than fifteen years.

Each day that I went to Rikers Island, I would have twenty-minute individual meetings with fifteen to twenty guys, which would start and end with a firm handshake. During these visits I would also bring them fiction and nonfiction book orders, fulfilling orders that had been placed on a previous visit.

After a day of meetings at Rikers, I would often reflect on the day on my drive home. I would feel a sense of reward, like I was doing important work that would have a long-term, positive effect on the guys. This work also gave me a great deal of satisfaction, and I looked ahead to the possibility of helping thousands of individuals in the years to come. To accomplish this, the next steps had to be set in motion. A structure had to be put into place to serve the guys once they were released. I needed to start spending more time in the city tending to important issues, including:

- Hire an office manager/assistant

- Develop a fundraising plan

- Assemble a board of directors

- Staff the agency with social workers

- Hire a finance director

- Hire an HR director

- Put an accounting firm, law firm, public relations agency, and lobbyist on retainer

I did not have sufficient funding, so I was going to be the "chief cook and bottle washer" for the foreseeable future. Once we received more funding, I would be able to think about staffing. I felt compelled to start this much-needed reentry agency as soon as possible to fill the great need I had uncovered. My entrepreneurial spirit drove me to work around the clock getting GOSO set up while I continued to visit Rikers and meet with the guys. While GOSO started out small, it grew fast, and by the time I retired fifteen years later, the number of guys who'd joined the program would reach close to ten thousand in total.

So how did my business background enable me to take on the above-mentioned aspects of the new organization without any funding? I worked around the clock. In my corporate career, I had already been exposed to every aspect of the new agency at one time or another. Everyone either reported directly to me or I had direct responsibility for their function. When I wasn't visiting Rikers Island, I would put on one of the many hats I had worn over the years and perform that function to build the agency. The process of starting GOSO had created a whole new life for me, and while I was starting a new beginning myself, I was witnessing the guys start their own new beginnings. There was one major difference between my many roles in the corporate world and the role I was playing in building an agency from the ground up. GOSO was all about saving lives, whereas my corporate roles had relied heavily on making profits.

There is a reason this chapter is titled, "It's All about the Guys." While simply stated, it is the root of all we do at GOSO, and I cannot tell you how many times I had to drive this point home with the staff, the board, funders, and every other facet of the agency.

Every time there was a discussion or conflict at GOSO, this statement served as a reminder for all involved and was quickly established as the theme of the agency. There were no exceptions, no matter how dire the circumstances that caused any conflict of interests. I was committed to GOSO putting the guys above everything else. It was not about me, not about the staff, not about the board of directors, not even about our funders; it was all about the guys, and I wanted everyone to be constantly advised of that fact. No exceptions.

Over the past sixteen years, I don't think there has been a single conflict that hasn't been resolved simply by inserting this concept into the conversation. All issues easily get settled when the guys are put first. Everybody either clicked with this concept or left the agency. I can't imagine any social service agency not having the exact same mantra.

People have been asking me for years why I didn't include women in the Getting Out and Staying Out program. I did make one trip to the Rose M. Singer Center (RMSC) on Rikers Island, which houses the female inmates. Truth be told, after spending a day there, I decided that I was never going to return. Those women had me for lunch. They were so much tougher than the guys and showed me very little respect. It also didn't help that I wasn't qualified to answer their questions. While they faced many of the same challenges as the men, their struggles were compounded by women's issues, which were more complex. Further, I felt that the presence of women in the program would be an added distraction for the guys.

# CHAPTER SIX

# The GOSO Guys Speak Out

*Showing gratitude is one of the simplest yet most*
*powerful things humans can do for each other.*
**—RANDY PAUSCH**

O ver the years, I found myself extremely impressed with the way the guys showcased their resilience, expressed their hopes and dreams, and openly listened to suggestions before following through with them. Because of the trust that had been built between us, the guys were able to express their gratitude for the unwavering support that GOSO has continued to give them over the years. They were especially appreciative because they had never received support like this before.

Can you imagine growing up without consistent support from your family and friends? These guys didn't receive suggestions or guidance regarding their future, hopes, and dreams until they came to GOSO.

What you are about to read are seven letters from GOSO guys. Some are still incarcerated, and others have been released. For sixteen years, I have had the privilege of meeting and working with these men, along with ten thousand of their brothers.

I have known John, Carlos, Miliki, Manny, and Anton for at least ten years, and others for as long as fifteen years. I first met them on Rikers Island, continued working with them during their incarceration. I've worked with some of them for as long as twelve years, and I am still working with several as their coach/mentor now that they have been released. Unfortunately, Burnell and Johnny are still up top, serving time.

Needless to say, one does not get into the social service world to receive accolades from the people whom they are serving. However, should you decide to make this move, you will learn that these types of letters and calls will inspire you to continue working with participants while they are still in your basic program. If you are anything like me, you will also look forward to hearing from them once they have moved on and matured into successful business leaders, entrepreneurs, and family members. Whenever I receive correspondence or calls from any of them, it makes my day.

Excited for your next project, A brief recap- We met on rikers, beacon 2005. I graduated valedictorian with your help and got a high school diploma. I plead guilty and took ten years. Got my bachlors from ohio state and came home to now getting my MBA at rutgers. Along the way i built www.emmaspremiumservices.com and landed on forbes. The company is $1 Million + in sales this year and I am finally off parole. You played a huge part in my life and I hope you know I owe a lot of where i am today cause of you.

My time up top was spent earning credits towards my bachlors. I spent some time in solitary where I learned spanish and taught myself to read russian, I also wrote a business plan for Emmas which today has sales exceeding $1M.

I graduated eventually prior to coming home and enrolled into rutgers MBA program.

I did 98 months up top and came home when I was 26 years old.

ANTON

*"The company is $1 Million + in sales this year and I am finally off parole. You played a huge part in my life and I hope you know I owe a lot of where I am today cause of you."*

Monday, February 15, 2021

Dear Mr. Goldsmith,

I pray that this letter finds you in the best of health and strength during these times and circumstances. I would like to say thank you first and foremost for the date book in which was well received. Presently, I am going through the motions and trying to be encouraged with under the covid memorandums; although, they change from day to day I cannot complain because an once of prevention is worth a pound of cure. You get the gist of the pressures! So, much is going on and I know that you can't reach out within a moments time and the postal service is at an all time disfunction. Nonetheless, I am grateful for even you taking the time to reach out even when you should be enjoying your retirement. All in all I thank you.

In lighter news, I know that you're as much old-school as I am with technology and snail mail; however, Jpay has now afforded most of NYS DOCCS with an email platform for sake of time an convenience if you so wish. Nevertheless, I don't mind the pen/ keys to the page style as you for it feel much more personal and sincere, but if need be for the sake of time the option is there whenever you so choose, okay Mr. G. Often times I feel so ashamed to be reminded of your continuity to even out work me at such a young age of 83. Most importantly, if it ever when unsaid, but truly you are the longest friendship and the biggest inspiration in which I try to model my life around because as you can see currently we're highly shore on people of good character and integrity. Mr. G., for many years I've searched and studied many subject matters and thought under so many but none could ever measure up to those Rikers Island years and those one-on-one times that still means more to me than the almost 20 years combined...and I can't say thank you enough for seeing "that" something in me that honestly I didn't even see in myself.

Respectively, regarding the book, I think that eventhough it may seem as a working title the main objective is the work that was put in and the vast results that came out. I certainly have been given a front row seat to what hard work and dedication looks like from one of the most selfless human being I've ever met along my 38 year journey on this earth. Some have talked it but none have shown it with or by better grace. I know that time isn't a luxury to us but I wholeheartedly one day hope the see you once again face to face my dear friend and finally putting the last period to this chapter on my book

# BURNELL

"I certainly have been given a front row seat to
what hard work and dedication looks like."

Saturday, November 29, 2020

Dear Mr. Goldsmith,

How have you been doing? Sincerely, I pray that these words finds you in the best of health and strength under this most uncertain time in the daily going's of our life with this pandemic. It seems a bit unheard of that just a few years ago life was going to and fro without the slightest thought of covid-19; nonetheless, here we stand with all of life's new normal. Overall, I'm glad to have built such a life-long friendship that goes beyond what mere words can ever express to you Mr. Mark L. Goldsmith. With some almost 20 years knowing each other but I still can get myself to call you by your first name without the formal address so please forgive any misplaced sentiments, okay. Most importantly, I ptay that you and your family are doing well.

I am a bit disheartened by the news of your retirement; however, I am most honored because it could not have happened to a more better man Mr. Goldsmith. Moreover, I think that the young men who have had the opportunity of meeting you are much better men now than ever. You have sure left a big impact on my life that at times I still believe that I've met the real MJ of my lifetime. In addition, I'm looking forward to your written words because I've been stuck for quite some time now trying to figure out how to flip the re-start switch. With that said I truly apologize about the long gap in my reaching out but I have become so consumed with so much self-guilt and fallen into a downward spiral mentally. I know that I should be upbeat amidst such uncertain times and trust me I'm taking it second by second at best for now.

On another note, I have since received a letter in support of my being granted clemency by the victim of my case sister. With the already pending application being sent 2 years now and I am at a loss of words, I know that my letter is short and but brief but I pray that your spirit is lifted upon hearing from me.

BURNELL

*"I think the young men who have had the opportunity of meeting you are much better men now than ever."*

I first met Mark Goldsmith, Mr. G., at Horizon Academy in Riker's Island 16 years ago when I was 19. GOSO was nothing more than an idea when we conversed during the few times we met.

I continued to meet with Mr. G. the entire time I was at the facility housing the school, becoming involved in GOSO at its infant stages as a result. Though I was transferred to a different holding facility shortly after meeting him, he promised me we would never lose contact. He kept his promise.

My first month upstate - after a 2 month stint in reception[1] - I wrote to Mr. G., thanking him for his thoughtful guidance and moral support. He wrote back reminding me of his pledge to remain in contact. A few weeks later I received an application from Ohio University to enroll in college. He even remembered how passionate I was about going to college and continuing my education. And as GOSOs first participant, I eventually enrolled in correspondence courses financially supported by Mr. G.

Less than a month after receiving my courses, Mr. G. sent me a typewriter for me to do homework on.

We would communicate by phone and via mail every few months or so to send updates: I about school and he about GOSO. Through our communication I got to witness GOSO evolve from a great idea, to an office in some random building, and finally to a storefront location in Harlem.

I was constantly made aware of participants' progress and success stories. I always felt a part of whatever was going on despite my distance from it all.

A few days after reentering society, I called Mr. G. to set up a meeting. We met a week or so later due to him being in Washington D.C. fighting the good fight. When we finally met, he proudly introduced me to everyone and made me feel very welcomed by the GOSO family. That same day I was invited to speak at an annual fundraising event happening a few weeks later.

At that event I met with most staff members and most of the administrators that helped make GOSO a successful and reputable program alongside Mr. G. After telling a little bit of my story to everyone in attendance at the event, a man by the name of Ira Wachtel engaged me in conversation. He became very interested about my current outlook on life and how I planned on moving forward after my devastating ordeal. Like Mr. G., Ira is strong proponent of giving people a fair shot at life. We conversed that evening and became good friends as a result. So much so that he introduced me to his daughter, Erika Weinstein, who eventually interviewed me for a position at her company and hired me on the spot. She gave me my first shot at corporate

---

[1] Reception in this instance is a holding facility for newly minted prisoners preparing to do serious time in an upstate correctional institution.

America and I am forever indebted to her for doing so. Ira was and continues to be interested in my growth and success.

After the fundraising event, Mr. G., Ira and I remained in contact and met on various occasions for dinner and the occasional cigar. Ira always made it his business to make sure I was invited to any event held for or by GOSO. And just like they had asked me before, I was invited to speak once again at the annual fundraising event they held at one of the board member's home in 2018.

The last time Mr. G. and I met was at the Apollo Theater a few weeks ago from the penning of these words. He invited me and a small group of GOSO guys to see Latin History for Morons after dinner. We all then went backstage to meet John Leguizamo and immortalized the moment with a photograph. I suspect the next time Mr. G., Ira and I meet again it will involve a good cigar and an even better conversation.

I arrived 8/2003
We met 4/2004
I went up top 7/2004
I was in 6 different facilities
I was released 9/2017

# CARLOS

*"I suspect that the next time Mr. G, Ira and I meet again it will involve a good cigar and an even better conversation."*

Dear Mr. G.                                    5/27/2021

I am so honored to be placed in your memoire. I am so excited by being apart of that. I won't ever tell you no. Your my mentor, role model and father figure. You have helped me over the years mature into the man I am today. If it wasn't for you to push me in my education. I don't believe I will be where I am today. As you may know, I am still currently enrolled in John Jay College and Hostos Community College.

JOHNNY R.

*"You have helped me over the years to mature into the man I am today."*

When I was incarcerated on Rikers Island GRVC in 2005 while attending the GED program their Horizon Academy. I was introduced to a great man, mentor, coach, and friend by the name of Mark Goldsmith, who had a program call GOSO. The requirements were to submit a resume and a story about yourself. Mark would meet with inmates, once a week at the school to discuss what was waiting for us when we got out. He was teaching us about the recidivism rate, and many useful information about vocational trainings, educational programs, that GOSO would assist in paying. The approach to re enter society in a productive way.

I took full advantage of what GOSO had to offer from day one. Mark Goldsmith met with me one on one every week and provided assistance with communication with my attorney, and district attorneys from the courts. To help me get the best possible outcome. This was vital when a youngman growing raised in a low poverty neighborhood where most either get killed or end up in prison with no resource from inside or assistance financially. Thanks to Mark, I received a great offer, instead of more prison time which is common under the circumstances. Instead, I was offer an impatient rehabilitation program, where I obtained a vocational training, my commercial drivers licensr. I attended intervention groups. I learned how to become a responsible independent youngman living on my own.

I had to meet certain requirements in order to be released and have my case dismissed. Get a trade, complete all levels of the treatment program. Save 2,000, find a my own place and successfully pass my GED.

I took my GED exam four times, I could not pass for nothing no matter how much I studied. I had met all the other requirements but the GED was my challenge. I needed help in convincing the court this was psychological, requesting they release me since progress was being made. Everytime I took the exam and failed I had too wait three months to re take it.

Mark Goldsmith stepped in and reached out to the Drug Czar of NYC. He fought with them to get the point. Not everyone is a good test takers. I was one of them.

While in the GOSO program I met with Mark Goldsmith every week like we were still at Rikers. He mentored me every step of the way. Provided money for transportation, clothes for interviews. How to negotiate salary reviews, how to speak during interviews. Mark was very influential anytime I needed something.

I completed the treatment program. 5% success rate. I obtained my commercial driver's license. Became gainfully employed. I got married had a child. Bought my first house at the age of twenty three. Making 45,000 a year, had my whole entire life transformed in a matter of four years.

Currently, I am living in Pennsylvania. My son is 12 years old. I have my own business. Working as a Safety Consultant for three trucking companies making 58,000 a year.

It's been 1⁄ years since I met Mark Goldsmith. We have conversations frequently. Mark Goldsmith has been a HUGE part of my future and still remains a big part of my life. I am humble to have a met such a great role model to be apart of such a great program with a great cause.
Thank you Mark for all you have done. I will always be forever thankful.

WE NEED MORE PEOPLE LIKE MARK!!!!!!!

JOHN G.

*"I learned how to become a responsible independent young man living on my own."*

I remember it like it was yesterday, the year was 2007 and i got arrested in my senior year of high school, a few months before graduation, all i could think was i just threw my life away i have to do time and i will never get to graduate from high school or college. Then one day i was in my cell on Rikers Island and a guard informed me that I could go to school in jail" i was like school in jail" really? i was extremely excited not only was i excited that i could restart my life i was happy to get out of the cell. On the first day of school we walked into a real classroom setting that was setup inside the prison, it had desks, chalk boards and even outside teachers who were not prison guards. and one day while I was attending school mr. goldsmith came in as a guest speaker, they would have different people come in from time to time to talk to us and inspire us, but out of all speakers that i met during this sentence i knew mr.goldsmith was genuine, you could tell by his aura and how he dealt with the students. He told us the students about the program he was starting called getting out and staying out and that's exactly what i wanted, to get out and stay out ! so i would always strike conversations with him so he would know i was serious and so he would accept me into the program upon my release, he would always give me a few minutes and give me respect as a human being he didnt treat me like a inmate and thats another thing i loved about him. they say you can judge a mans character by how he treats people who can do nothing for him. so based on the way he treated me i knew he had great character . fast forward a few months later i got sentenced and was about to be shipped upstate to finish my time. i informed mr. goldsmith and he told me to stay in contact with him, so i did, i wrote him and he wrote me back. my girlfirend even stopped writing me so for mr goldsmith to write me it make me feel specail because it gave me hope to know that someone believed in me and wanted to see me do good. in return thats exactly what i did like a son and a father i would constanlty keep him updated on the steps i was taking to get my life back in order i wanted to make him proud and he always let me know he was proud of me and that kept me going. upon my release i enrolled in college, lehman college and majored in business. i maintaind a 3.5 gpa and got A++'s in all  my business classes . i Also worked full-time as a dishwasher to keep myself busy and to stay out of trouble and to let mr goldsmith know that all of the effort he put into me wasnt in vein. fast forward a few years later i entered into a business pitch competition and i came in first place out of fifty other men. i won a office space for a year, startup money and free business assistance. with that i started my compnay i-haul-junk,inc and not only did i quit my job but i hired other men that were fresh out of prison. which i learned from Mr. Goldsmith no matter how "high up" you get you should always give back and extend your hand to those who truly need it. Lastly mr. Goldsmith was one of my first customers. He hired me to remove some items out of his home on Park avenue. Mr. Goldsmith was a real life changer for me and I will forever be grateful for the time and energy ʋe put into me . Thank you Mr. Goldsmith.

Good Afternoon, Mr. Goldsmith.

i⸳ ⸳ ⸳ ⸳, my team and I just completed the move and removal of all items from 1400 5th Ave and 75 E 116th. It was successful everything is cleared out and we donated a ton of items to participants and other non-profit location which we provided your team donation receipts for. Your new staff is amazing they were very kind and welcoming and it was a pleasure working with them. Thank you big time for the referral. This project helped us I-Haul-Junk,INC. Start the year off right . When your done with your book please reserve 10-20 copies for me and also I still owe you lunch, I'm ready when you are . Have a blessed Saturday . Thanks for everything !

. I wanted to update you on where I am at today. My fiancé and I just got approved for a mortgage, we fixed our credit saved some money and are now about to be home owners, we are actively house shopping and plan to close on something before July. We are buying a multifamily home, we are going to live in one unit and rent the others to help pay the ⸳ ⸳ ⸳

MALIKI

*"They say you can judge a man's character by how he treats people who can do nothing for him."*

Good morning Mr. G, good to hear from you this Sunday morning. It is an honor to be a part of your history and be mentioned in your book. What a pleasure.

I was first sent to the Vernon C. Bain Center " the Boat" in the Bronx on April 29th, 2003 after my arrest. I spent six months there then transferred to GMDC on October 13th, 2003. I was enrolled in the GED program at Horizon Academy a month later, November. I believe I met you in January. I was sent to Downstate on September 6th, 2004. Then transferred to Sing Sing on October 26th, 2004. I did my entire sentence at Sing Sing simply by staying out of trouble and joining every academic program available. After 16 years and eight months, I was finally released from Sing Sing on December 12th, 2019, six months earlier than my scheduled release date due to earning my Masters degree. Hope this was helpful. Please feel free to ask me any more questions if need be. Thanks.

On Sun, Oct 18, 2020 at 11:00 AM <mark.goldsmith936@gmail.com> wrote:

I remained in constant communication with Mr. Gold smith via mail. I would write a letter to Mr. G, to continue receiving guidance and good news from GOSO. Mr. G sent me Newsletters from GOSO to keep me informed about the successes of the program. The good news and updates made me happy and glad about Mr. G's great work. I was always excited to hear that he was reaching so many individuals.

Sure why not. I'm currently working for NYC Health and Hospitals as a case investigator in the Test & Trace Corp. Its working remotely so I enjoy the fact that I can work from the comfort of my own home. It's a great experience with good pay and great benefits. My family members are all doing well thank God. Andrew is 18 years old and attending BMCC. He wants to study forensic science. It has been wonderful for me. I'm looking forward to soon getting more opportunities to demonstrate my skills and prove that men like me deserve a good shot at being great citizens. I thank you both for always believing in me and trusting me.

# MANNY

*"I thank you both for always believing in me and trusting me."*

January 5, 201

Dear Mr. B,

Hey, I received your letter & planner today. Thank yo
for the planner and HAPPY BIRTHDAY to you and even tha
you turned 80 you still moving strong and look and good
doing my friend. Congratulations! I know your organizatic
is going to do well. What a blessing it is for those guys to l
a person like you in their corner for support. Remember
you can't help those, who don't want to help themselves. Te'
Ms. Ortiz congrats for me what a big step in her career c
I am so proud of her achievements. That was a beautifully
article it was heart touching to know that there are guys
there leading by example. As for me, I am enrolled with Jo
Jay College Prison-To-College Pipeline. I have 13 credits now
I am still fighting for a SARA-Compliant residence. I just got
latest address denied by Orange County, not parole. My mot
moved up to Newburgh and is there waiting for me to come hon
but today I got a notice by my counselor that the county he
refused my address. My mother has been trying everythin
in her power to get me released, but for one reason or anot
I continue to get denied. My parole office Mr. Fitzpatrick
Manhattan Area VII office # ████████████ was being hard o
me and didn't want to place in a shelter or at Ward's Island, sc
moved up to Newburgh. Now Newburgh county clerks office
guess was the ones that denied my address. I really don't
know what's going on right now. I am so stressed out and
crushed, I got no more tears left. My mother is crying, stress

and with limited funds things are hard. I have had 6 address denied already. My mother has lost so much money trying put down payments on apts, to only later get denied. All want is one chance to prove myself that I have changed me life around. I know I made a mistake and a poor decision, b I am tired of people judging me for my past. I want people t see my hard work and my determination to succeed in li I have done so much positive things with my life now. I have t get that second chance, something has to give man. I am s focused on reintegrating back into society and ready to wor to prove myself, but then I get slapped in the face with a deni I am eleven months past my release date now. I am trying stay strong but this is getting played out now. I need to get home to help my mother who is fighting breast cancer. Listen, look forward to your response letter, I got to go caused Ic get to emotional & crying right now. Thank you again for a that you do & continue to do for me and those who are just like me. Tell those guys to stay focused, keep their eyes o the prize and prove those that don't ~~believe in~~ us wrong. To it for me a fellow brother struggling to get out the system would love to do a motivational speech or talk to the young fellaz' in your program if possible. Mr. 6, it's always a pleasure to hear from you, you put a smile on my face even time I receive a letter from you. I know you believe in me an for that I thank you my friend. I love you geniunely & sincerel

JOHNNY R.

*"Tell those guys to stay focused, keep their eyes on the prize and prove those that don't believe in us wrong."*

63

# CHAPTER SEVEN

# The Three *E*'s: Education, Employment, and Emotional Well-Being

*The trouble with most of us is that we would rather
be ruined by praise than saved by criticism.*
**—NORMAN VINCENT PEALE**

Establishing primary objectives for its clients is the most important decision a not-for-profit has to make. It is vital that those objectives are measurable so that when grants are requested from both private and government sources, the agency can present their results in a timely and accurate fashion, justifying the funds while securing future funding. For GOSO, it was even more important that the guys realized their full potential and felt good about their ability to move forward in their lives.

**Establishing primary objectives for its clients is the most important decision a not-for-profit has to make.**

Coming from a corporate background, I had been producing measurable objective reports for over thirty-five years, so I knew how to impress funders with results from the get-go. It was an area that GOSO excelled in and allowed us to get impressive funding in our early years. With respect to the actual reports and measurements that I reported to funders, I naturally focused on our mission statement's objectives. I reported on a monthly basis the specifics of our recidivism rates; our education achievements, both GEDs and high school diplomas; and employment figures.

Most importantly, GOSO has maintained a clear focus on what the agency stands for. While the description has been refined over the years, the three pillars have remained the same.

## EDUCATION, EMPLOYMENT, AND EMOTIONAL WELL-BEING

We believed that as long as the GOSO guys focused on these three pillars, they would stay out of the criminal justice system while achieving educational heights, meaningful employment, and financial independence.

What makes GOSO truly unique is our emphasis on emotional well-being. Well over 50 percent of the young men whom I first met on Rikers Island had mental health issues. The educational and employment segments are easily characterized, whereas emotional well-being is more challenging to define. It was for this reason, as previously stated, that we only hired social workers with a master's in social work (MSW). In addition to being able to provide therapeutic intervention, trained social workers understand the concepts and scope of criminalization and mass incarceration, the impact on the young men and their families, and the social justice implications of their actions. Someone with an MSW is skilled in the foster care system, and they have tools for working through the trauma associated with those who have spent many years in the system, which made up a large percentage of the GOSO guys.

Over the years, we had MSW interns whom we trained in the fashion that we'd deemed necessary to work with formerly incarcerated young men and later hired them. The interns were able to sharpen their skills while they worked in that position and were well prepared for the full-time role of MSW at GOSO.

While prioritizing the emotional well-being of the GOSO guys was a major focus, it became clear that educational achievement was the key to their eventual success in the world. Many of them did not have a high school diploma of any sort. To achieve this success, the guys needed to start with a formal education, followed by on-the-job training, as well as specific training in social media and other necessary technological skills.

When I first met the guys on Rikers Island, many of them did not have a high school education. They were attending Horizon Academy, a District 79 school, which is part of the alternative school system of New York City, where a student can earn either a high school diploma or GED credentials.

One of the positives of my lecturing on Rikers Island was that the guys loved hearing my personal stories. I don't think they realized that successful businessmen like myself also had their fair share of problems, and the fact that I was willing to share those stories with them was a unique experience.

My own educational track is checkered, to say the least. I was a good athlete in high school, not a very good student. I was accepted into Penn State because I was a resident of Pennsylvania. After two years, the dean called me into his office and told me that one of us had to leave Penn State, and it obviously was not going to be him. I realized that I had just flunked out. Needless to say, the guys loved that story, since it mirrored many of their own educational experiences.

I then went into the US Navy because military service was mandatory in those days. After two years' active duty, I came to New York and met my future wife, who was getting her master's in social work at Columbia University. She suggested strongly that I return to college. I knew I could do the work and do it well, but I had just never applied myself to school.

I kept my full-time job and entered NYU, majoring in political science. In knew that I wanted to go to a graduate school of business, but I didn't want to spend all of my years in college studying business. While working full time, I graduated from college at the age of twenty-seven, then achieved my MBA at the Zicklin School of Business at Baruch College at the age of thirty.

The guys saw this as inspiration and quickly learned that it wasn't too late for them to finish high school and go on to a community college where they could do well and then transfer to a four-year school. Hundreds of GOSO guys did just that.

At Horizon Academy on Rikers Island, I brought many interesting, high-profile visitors to the school to talk to the students. Senator Cory Booker of New Jersey was one of those visitors who will certainly be remembered by the guys.

While leading a classroom discussion, Senator Booker learned that one of the students was interested in becoming a boxer, so he asked the young man what kind of shape he was in and how many push-ups he could do. The young man said fifty and then proceeded to demonstrate his strength. Senator Booker took off his jacket and did seventy-five, challenging the young man not to underestimate his capabilities. In response, the aspiring boxer pumped out one hundred push-ups, proving that he could do even more than the fifty he originally limited himself to. The senator then addressed a couple hundred guys in an auditorium, challenging them to attend school while incarcerated. He followed this up by inviting them to make serious plans for their eventual return to society by pursuing the GOSO reentry plan.

When it came time to establish the GOSO program, I was immediately concerned about what would happen to the education of the men once they were released. While challenging, I felt that my only solution would be to ask for my own District 79 site on location at GOSO. Since we were doing so well with the guys inside Rikers Island, which was not an easy location to hold students' attention, I was granted my request. This would enable GOSO guys to see their social worker and attend school in the same location.

Once the school was opened, we continued to bring high-profile personalities, such as New York Yankees Hall of Famer Mariano Rivera, to speak with the guys. His talk with them was characterized by the concept of focusing on one thing at a time.

While speaking to the guys, Rivera cupped his hands around his eyes and told them that when he was facing really tough batters, he focused solely on his catcher, Jorge Posada's mitt. This helped him avoid being distracted by the high-profile batter, putting the ball exactly where his catcher wanted it. He asked the guys to only focus on one important aspect of the situation when they were faced with a dilemma.

Much in the same way that Rivera taught the guys to focus, I taught them about the importance of sticking with a regimented schedule that would help them succeed in the job market. If the guys were going to be ready to apply for jobs, they needed to be well equipped with the proper tools, which was why we created a mandatory, rigorous two-week Job Readiness Curriculum. Classes were held every day from ten to two, with lunch included.

Preparation, above all else, was the main hindrance when it came to the guys getting jobs, and the Job Readiness Curriculum provided them with coaching on the application process, interviewing skills, and follow-up.

Week one started with an orientation and then a review of their basic computer skills, which they needed to apply for jobs. We then focused on effective workplace habits and the first phase of the job search process. The guys needed jobs as soon as possible, so we didn't have time to waste. Resume writing and advanced, effective workplace habits were the first part of the week-one agenda, followed by the review of educational and vocational programs available in the city. The guys learned how to conduct an independent job search, and by the end of the first week, they were using the skills they learned in mock interviews where they had to prepare and answer all the questions posed to them. When it came to writing resumes and cover letters, few of the guys recognized how much work they had already done before they started to put it all down on paper, and many of them had never heard of the all-important cover letter.

Their biggest deficiency was that their self-esteem was at zero; hence their inability to talk positively about themselves once the question and answer period was over. Once again I stepped in with my corporate experience and relayed the following story to them:

When I was twenty-nine years old, not that much older than most of them, I was working in sales in the Garment District, making $6,000 a year. I saw an ad run by the Pfizer corporation that had just acquired a cosmetic company called Coty, and they were looking for a sales administrator, paying $12,000 a year, twice what I was making. I told myself there was nothing to lose, so I went for the job and got it. But that was not the end of the story. Within two years I was promoted to the marketing department, which was my initial goal. According to management, I was offered the promotion because I had just led the best sales meeting that they'd ever had. At the meeting announcing my promotion, I asked the head personnel guy why he had hired me in the first place. He told me that he was impressed in my first interview when I told him I would be going for my MBA in marketing at night while maintaining my job at Coty during the day.

He was so impressed that he not only hired me but said that Pfizer would pay for graduate school if I maintained a B+ average. They were all very impressed that I was able to succeed in doing that while I was working full time for Pfizer, working during the day and attending night school four times a week at NYU.

My message to the guys was for them to put their fear aside during the interview process and share whatever positive achievements or potential advances they were making in education and training and to make sure they showed enthusiasm for the job. I further suggested that they not be afraid to ask for the best possible salary, which they just might get if the interviewer is as impressed with them as the Pfizer guy was with me. The job at Pfizer launched my twenty-five-year career in cosmetics. All this was because I informed the interviewer that I would be going to graduate school at night for an MBA in marketing that would enhance my career opportunities.

There was a very small dropout rate after the first week of the curriculum; however, once the participants found out that we would not send them out on interviews without their completing the second week, the bulk of them returned and finished the curriculum.

This was yet another example of the basic philosophy of GOSO. We were not going to spend our valuable time and funding on young men who were not doing their part. They had to be stepping up and committing themselves to full participation in the program at all times. While the program didn't cost them money, they quickly learned that it was not a free ride, and they were required to do their part if they wanted to succeed at turning their lives around.

The week ended with a curriculum review of everything they had covered in the first week.

The second week of the program featured career exploration. Most of them didn't have an answer when we asked them what they would be interested in doing for a living, and many of them had never been asked the question. They had only been told what to do, where to go, and what their limited options were.

We then put them back on the computer to learn the basic skills that they would need to effectively use the internet for job searches and career exploration.

Next on the program were internships and employment essentials that they needed to understand. Most of them had never had a job on the books; rather, they had been paid in cash for odd jobs with no benefits, no 401(k), and no vacations.

Time management was next on the agenda. When asked about their time, they all thought that they were very busy until they were forced to write down what they had actually done hour by hour for a full week. Only then did they realize how much time they had been wasting.

Before they could go through the final curriculum review, they had to pass an interview with me, where I tested them thoroughly on all the covered subjects. Those who didn't pass the interview test were required to spend the week sharpening their knowledge on the topics before they could proceed. Part of the interview test was looking the part, and they were responsible for setting up an appointment with my secretary and then showing up at my office with a knock on the door, dressed in a shirt and tie, and introducing themselves with a firm handshake. GOSO maintains a clothing closet full of proper interview attire, including a great selection of ties.

Graduates of the job readiness program were awarded certificates, and qualified candidates were sent out on interviews that they had either found on their own or were developed by our job-search group. We expanded the job readiness program and developed a milestone program, which provided incentives for members when they graduated from one level to the next.

The levels were: entry level, full participant, advanced participant, and alumni participant. Additional milestones that were incentive motivated included: complete community supervision ($250.00); earn high school diploma or equivalency ($250.00); complete trade school and receive diploma ($350.00); and earn a college degree ($500.00). As a former corporate sales/marketing executive, I had learned that there was nothing wrong with incentives; they motivated people to do the right thing for themselves and for the company they worked for.

The intent was for GOSO guys not to leave the program but to remain in contact for years, which is what they have done by becoming part of the alumni, similar to what college students do. "Once a GOSO guy, always a GOSO guy," was another one of our mottos.

One of the GOSO guys whom I have known for over sixteen years, Manny, graduated at the head of his class on Rikers Island, went upstate, where he earned college degrees, and has since returned to the city. At his high school graduation on Rikers Island, his three-year-old son attended.

Manny was later quoted as saying:

My family members are all well, thank God. My son is now eighteen years old and attending community college. He wants to study forensic science. I am looking forward to getting more opportunities to demonstrate my skills and prove that men like me deserve a good shot at being great citizens.

I thank you for always believing in me and trusting me.

One aspect of GOSO that differs from most social service agencies is that our services are available to them years after they leave the formal training segment. For GOSO members, finding their first job is only the first step in their achieving financial independence. They need continued guidance on how to move up in a company, how to ask for a raise, how to deal with conflicts with their supervisors, as well as how to deal with any diversity issues that they might run into, since most of them are men of color.

GOSO has most recently established a coaching club that graduates participate in. Since young executives their age are being coached in their corporate careers, why shouldn't GOSO guys be afforded the same opportunity?

John, whom I coach, has been in the trucking world, working off the books and without benefits for years. He was recently offered a position with a major blue-chip corporation as a driver, where he would receive benefits and an IRA. He took the job, and no more than three months later, his former employer called him back and asked him to return to his previous position with a huge raise, benefits, and an opportunity to learn more about the inner workings of the company. Needless to say, he accepted the offer and is now being compensated in the six figure range.

What has always fascinated me is the entrepreneurial spirit of the GOSO guys and their willingness to take the time to learn a business before trying to start their own businesses. As a regular practice, I review business plans that they have put together, and I usually end up telling them that they are not ready, as they haven't taken into consideration the many pitfalls that would stop them from succeeding. The good news is they do persevere and, in most cases, end up starting a successful business.

There was another initiative that I started on Rikers Island that I continued once we opened our offices. The guys' use of negative words to describe their color had to stop, and while I recognized that it was a way for them to communicate in a "wise guy" kind of way, I thought that it was also a sign of disrespect for each other and the community at large. This was not any easy undertaking, but I was determined to stop the use of those words in and around GOSO. When the guys eventually realized that I was really serious about this, they adapted. Needless to say, I was hoping that they would take that lesson learned at GOSO back to their neighborhoods and institute it with their friends and family. Because of how society had referred to them from the day they were born, it was easy to understand how and why they used the term. On further reflection, I believe that most of them understood exactly why I would not tolerate it in the office, and if they continued to use the terms, they would be asked to not only leave the office but also potentially be asked to take a short leave of absence from GOSO.

# CHAPTER EIGHT

# Finding a Location
# and Hiring

*Continuous effort—not strength or intelligence—*
*is the key to unlocking your potential.*
**—WINSTON CHURCHILL**

Working out of Starbucks was fine when first starting GOSO; however, as the number of guys being seen upon their release from Rikers grew, a real office to work out of was needed for many reasons. The primary need was for privacy so the guys would feel that they could speak frankly about their situations and get advice from our staff of social workers.

Of paramount importance to me was that I wanted the office to be a welcoming site so that the guys would feel comfortable coming there and being open to our program once they committed themselves to making dramatic changes to their lives.

GOSO guys have never felt comfortable in formal offices for several reasons. Many times they had been called into those types of offices to be reprimanded, dismissed, or criticized in one way or another. Further, most of the living circumstances that they grew up in were characterized by overcrowding, in communities that were drug and gun infested.

I was committed to having that first GOSO office be a beautiful, clean, well-furnished, tasteful place that did not require a lot of funds.

Rather than having my own office, I created a workspace and conference room all in one. This enabled me to have my privacy when I needed it and have all important meetings take place in the same room by simply moving my chair from my desk to the conference table.

All of the social workers had their own spaces to ensure privacy when they were working with the guys, and administrative workers all shared workspaces.

I had met most of the guys on Rikers Island so that when they saw me, a friendly face, they immediately felt more relaxed than they might have felt walking into a strange, new office.

At this time I was still using my own money to fund my transportation to Rikers Island, books for the guys, and other ancillary expenses. As an entrepreneur, I had been through these times before while setting up my own corporation, IMS. Fortunately, my wife was also a professional and a wage earner.

I also made sure that all of my GOSO guys urged their significant others to seek employment if they planned on living in New York City, simply because it is incredibly difficult to make it in the city on one salary. I had been in this position early on in my marriage, and I passed this experience on to them because I wasn't sure they would receive proper advice from anyone else. The guys always appreciated when I shared my real life experiences with them, and their willingness to listen justified my decision to do just that.

Once I established the office logistics, I started to approach foundations to raise money specifically to fund the opening of the needed office. My prayers were answered when a foundation agreed to a $25,000 grant that would be used to help fund a new office. Over fifteen years later, that foundation remains a key funder of GOSO. I have always been focused on not only reaching out to new funding sources but also on cultivating existing funders with the positive results that come from their funding.

**The guys always appreciated when I shared my real life experiences with them, and their willingness to listen justified my decision to do just that.**

The actual search for the office was not an easy one for one specific reason. When landlords found out that we would be working with formerly incarcerated young men, they found a reason to deny me a lease. They did not want my guys in their hallways and/or elevators. A solution needed to be found, and once again the fact that I used my entrepreneurial skills enabled me to find a simple solution immediately. An office would have to be found in a storefront that required no travel through hallways or on elevators of a building.

Rather than using a real estate agent or the newspaper, I realized that I had to do the search on my own. I wanted to find an office in Harlem, close to the Triborough Bridge that led to Rikers Island. Walking north from my residence on East 94th Street, I paid particular attention to two-way streets, knowing that those types of streets also had better lighting and transportation and would be near subway stops. I found an empty storefront on East 116th Street between Park and Madison Avenues, one block from the Lexington Avenue subway and two blocks from the Seventh Avenue Line. It was the perfect spot.

I called the owner's telephone number on the front door, and when I told her that we wanted the office, I was relieved that I received an immediate positive response. We set up a meeting for the next day to meet with my son, at that time a real estate lawyer. He brought a letter of intent for both of us to sign, along with provisions for a security payment. I told the landlord that I was leaving for Russia in three days for two weeks. I sketched out exactly how I wanted the office redone, received her approval, and called a carpentry service that I had used before, drew up a floor plan, gave them the keys to the office, and they went to work. When I got back from Russia, the office was 100 percent ready to go. The landlord was so impressed by the work that we were doing with formerly incarcerated young men that she became a financial supporter of GOSO for years.

There was no time to waste. This entrepreneur wanted to get on with his work in a newly designed office that was a safe setting for the guys. It was very important to me that they felt safe and well respected, and I wanted to make sure they were listened to in a supportive fashion that gave them the feeling of trust and security. These were not the type of feelings that they had harbored in their lifetimes, either before or after they ended up on Rikers Island.

Next up was the hiring of an officer manager/assistant to run the office in my absence and assist me in the day-to-day operations. That search yielded an excellent candidate, Roberto, who happened to be Latinx and spoke Spanish, which was important since close to 50 percent of the guys were Latinx. He bonded well with the guys and stayed with me for years before leaving to successfully advance his own career. To this day, we continue to talk about the good old days when we first got started.

I immediately tasked the new employee with taking care of details such as phone, internet, and electric services, which he accomplished in record time. From the start I knew that I only wanted to hire people who could take direction and then work collaboratively to perform their tasks in a professional and timely fashion. We were going to be staffed sparsely, so it was important for everyone to pull their weight.

I also made the decision to never hire a client. I wanted the guys to be in the real world, finding jobs in the marketplace by being resourceful and creative on their own. Had I given them jobs at GOSO, I would have robbed them of the experience of finding work on their own. They appreciated my decision when I explained why I could not hire them.

That first office remained our only space for several years, until we grew to the point that we could no longer handle the number of guys that we were seeing on a daily basis. I had always coveted a corner space on the street, and as soon as I saw a rental sign go up down the street, I was there to contact the new landlord and rent the location. This space was even more beautiful, and most importantly, it was on the corner of 116th Street and Madison Avenue and was conveniently located with subway service on Lexington and bus service on both Madison and 5th Avenues. Madison Avenue was a major thoroughfare for drivers leaving Manhattan, driving north to Yankee Stadium and other sites, which raised awareness for GOSO. It organically created a billboard-like effect in plain view of all drivers, and soon GOSO was on the map.

GOSO has recently moved to a brand-new, greatly expanded, seventeen-thousand-square-foot office, including its own GED center onsite, which formerly was in a different location. My legacy lives on, carrying on the great traditions that allowed me to grow it from an idea on Rikers Island to Starbucks to a storefront in East Harlem to a major force in reentry in New York City. We never grew beyond our means, but I definitely moved ahead on a wing and a prayer when it came to expansion, as we needed the space to grow. It was quite a change from the Madison Avenue that I'd once known, when I worked in the glamorous advertising business before starting GOSO in East Harlem.

# CHAPTER NINE

# Board of Directors

*"A community is like a ship: everyone ought
to be prepared to take the helm."*
**—HENRIK IBSEN**

T he primary responsibilities of any board of directors include fiduciary responsibility, fundraising, overseeing the development of the agency, and building a strong relationship with the executive director or president of the organization. Developing a strong board of directors is critical to the operation of a nonprofit. My first step in developing GOSO's board was to put out the call to a select group of men and women to see who might be interested in becoming a charter board member.

Having served on several boards of directors in my lifetime, I had experienced both effective and ineffective boards. What characterized the best boards was a deep commitment to the mission of the organization and a willingness to spend time contributing both fiscally and with passion and dedicated time.

I was looking for a cross section of professionals who had a sincere interest and passion for reforming our criminal justice system, a system that had incarcerated 25 percent of the world's incarcerated population in a country that only had 5 percent of the world's total population. Most importantly, prospective board members had to have a strong belief in second chances for young men who were not as fortunate as they were, having typically grown up in poverty and on public assistance. Many of them were also part of the foster care system of New York City.

I reached out primarily to friends and business associates, both male and female, many of whom I had worked with for over thirty-five years in the corporate world as fellow workers, suppliers, and/or consultants. The response was phenomenal. Virtually no one turned me down.

I even recruited one of my most involved board members, Ira Wachtel, at a memorial service for a favorite uncle. In a letter addressed to me, a GOSO guy named Carlos mentioned Mr. Wachtel, who had been coaching him for over a year with outstanding results. Carlos was quoted as saying the following:

"At a GOSO event, I met a man named Mr. Wachtel who engaged me in conversation, as he became interested in my current outlook on life and how I planned on moving forward after my devastating ordeal. Like Mr. G., Mr. Wachtel is a strong proponent of giving people a fair shot at life." Ira's daughter Erika actually gave Carlos his first job in administration while he interned for a financial position in her company.

Here again is a great example of GOSO's desire to treat the young men in our program as if they were our own sons and entitled to the same advantages as we bestow on our own offspring.

Marketing, advertising, public relations, finance, law, education, social services, and human relations were the primary areas of influence and experience that I was searching for and found in our directors. Prospects that had the potential to be individual funders, as well as had friends and associates who were possible funders, were also given strong consideration. Willingness to work on committees and contribute to the annual benefit were also important ingredients required in their commitment to serve on the GOSO board of directors.

The GOSO board of directors was going to be more of an extension of myself for the first few years. None of them had any experience in the criminal justice field, and many of them didn't have previous experience serving on a board of directors. I was looking forward to the day when the board could participate more in mentoring the guys at GOSO by volunteering their services or bringing potential volunteers to broaden our awareness in New York City, and I wanted them to move beyond their fiduciary responsibility to actually get to know our clients.

Another one of my first board members, Richard Block, actually started coming to Rikers Island with me on a weekly basis and continued for several years. Richard, a former entrepreneur and now a retired investor, really enjoyed sitting down with guys individually and exposing them to the possibility of becoming entrepreneurs in their own right once released. I know of at least one situation where one of his students ended up doing just that in a very successful fashion.

What Richard was best at was listening to the guys express their hopes and dreams for entrepreneurship. Then he took what they said and brought a sense of reality to their plans, helping them to create business opportunities that had a good chance of succeeding.

Board member Charles Kushner was particularly sensitive to the needs of the guys. He ended up coming to Rikers Island with me on a weekly basis for over a year, working directly with the individual guys, planning what they might do once they were released. He mirrored what I had been doing from the day that I first entered Rikers while serving on the board of directors.

He didn't lecture them; rather, he spoke with them and showed them great respect, listening to their hopes and dreams of what their lives might be like when they were released. He quickly earned their respect not by touting his success but rather by listening to them. Most importantly, he recognized their untapped potential. He took copious notes to make sure that we had a record of what had transpired in their individual meetings so that anyone who followed him would have a history of his conversations with them. This was an entirely new experience in the guys' lives, where a successful businessman was talking to them and giving them advice on how to follow their dreams. Eventually he ended up hiring GOSO guys in his corporate entity, some who are still employed in his company years later.

He also then reached out to his family, and they supported GOSO in unique ways. His son Jared facilitated my appearance at the White House. And his son Josh created a very unique, high-tech program in which GOSO guys are given the opportunity to intern in preparation for achieving entry-level positions in the highly competitive, well-compensated technology industry.

Whenever I interviewed potential board members, I always emphasized that they would be responsible for reaching out to their circle of friends, family, and associates who might be willing to volunteer their services by exploring how to use their own professional experiences.

The examples set by Richard Block, Charles Kushner, and Ira Wachtel proved that getting family and friends involved in a program that betters society is always a good thing, and they used their expertise and connections to provide employment and set up opportunities for them.

Another person who joined the board was the premier hair stylist to high-profile Black entertainers in the music, theatre, and movie industry. John Atchison actually came to GOSO on a consistent basis, teaching styling to interested guys. He then took it a step further when he agreed to take an intern to his salon to teach him how to style hair. He did this all in his spare time, when he wasn't attending to his busy salon responsibilities on Madison Avenue. The young man eventually decided not to pursue a career as a stylist, but he learned a great deal about the operation of a salon and owning a business.

Approximately three years before I retired from GOSO, I put together a three-year financial plan so that once I left, there would be at least a footprint for the agency going forward. I called on another board member, Norm Merritt, and asked him if he would spearhead the effort with me. I was aware that he had extensive experience doing forecasting and planning in the corporate world, so it seemed logical to ask him to collaborate with me on this effort, and he agreed. The best news, in retrospect, was that GOSO made all of the numbers forecasted in that plan.

With reference to how many directors would be desirable for a new not-for-profit, I had thought that the number should be twenty-five at full strength, and that is exactly where the agency is today, with several charter members still on board. The number of board members is not nearly as important as it is for each member to participate in the agency's activities either by volunteering their time, raising money, or suggesting different resources.

We then created an advisory board of former board members who had either moved from NYC, retired, or decided they needed to spend all their time on their own investments.

As it is in most businesses, some directors did not work out along the way. One particular board member thought it was more about him than it was about the guys, so he was quietly asked to resign from the board.

A second board member was giving lectures on job procurement. He came to my office after a particularly disappointing class and told me that the guys were just not where he wanted them to be. I explained to him that if they were where he wanted them to be, they would not have been sent to Rikers Island in the first place. Needless to say, he did not stay on the board.

Finally, I wanted to have a board of directors that could relate to the staff so there would be a communication level that produced positive results by working closely together on projects while respecting each other's boundaries. Proof of that working was demonstrated when GOSO'S chairman of the board, Reg Andre, was first brought to a GOSO event by a former senior staff member.

In addition to the board of directors, there is also a proactive action board consisting of young professionals, which is sometimes referred to as the junior board of directors. Since they are closer in age to the GOSO guys, many of their conversations involving music, sports, and movies were amazing to listen to because they had the same favorites. In addition to participating in all of the agency's fundraising events, they also have their own fundraising events attended primarily by other young professionals who are friends or associates. Moving up to the regular board was always a possibility for them, and that has already happened.

The interviewing process for new board members is an ongoing operation that never stops. Due to attrition, there will always be vacancies that need to be filled. Whenever I met a volunteer, I always raised the possibility of them becoming a future board member at GOSO when a vacancy needed to be filled.

Needless to say, rigorous research was done by the board search committee on every prospective member before their candidacy was brought to the full board for a vote.

GOSO's board played a huge role in both fundraising and program participation and helped elevate it to the agency it is today. In retrospect, the one deficiency that we were never able to correct was our inability to recruit several "deep-pocket" members capable of contributing in the six figure range on a consistent basis. That would have put GOSO on sounder financial footing earlier in its history. The good news is that GOSO is currently doing extremely well without that type of funding, and if board members with greater financial abilities do show interest, as one has recently, it will put the agency on an even greater growth track, serving even more young men involved in the criminal justice system of NYC.

The GOSO board of directors consists of a diverse group of men and women. GOSO continues to interview new prospective members who can contribute financially and offer support for the various programs the agency undertakes.

# CHAPTER TEN

# Fundraising: Government-Foundations-Individuals-Benefits

*What we have before us are some breathtaking
opportunities disguised as insoluble problems.*
**—JOHN GARDNER**

The lifeblood of any not-for-profit agency is its ability to fundraise consistently, ensuring it can function in a secure fashion without cash flow problems. In order to accomplish this, there must be a clear statement of the agency's goals. What is its mission? What is its focus; what are the objectives that need to be accomplished, and how will the agency go about achieving them? What social problem will the agency be trying to help eradicate?

Proposals should be clear and focused and include the agency's detailed budgets with objectives and outcomes. In one of my earlier chapters, the word "passion" was used to describe the essential ingredient for success of a nonprofit organization. This passion must be front and center when fundraising for a cause comes into play. Whether the passion stems from helping populations who are deprived of their rights or of basic needs such as food, shelter, and quality medical and mental healthcare, finding the best approach to the funding source will always be the number-one goal.

**This passion must be front and center when fundraising for a cause comes into play. Whether the passion stems from helping populations who are deprived of their rights or of basic needs, finding the best approach to the funding source will always be the number-one goal.**

## GOVERNMENT

Let's begin with government funding. There are three sources, including city, state, and federal. A start-up not-for-profit agency should generally begin with city funding because it is the most approachable due to its proximity. The city is also the most likely to benefit because their inhabitants are on the receiving end of the funding that will improve their lives.

Gaining knowledge about the city government will be essential in determining which local agencies hold the purse strings for available funding. The most logical place to start would be the city council, followed by the mayor's office and city agencies.

I made a huge mistake in trying to take on government funding without hiring a lobbyist. I wasted countless days and months trying to do it on my own since I thought of myself as an entrepreneur, which I *was* in the corporate world. Government funding is very different from raising money or securing investors in the corporate world. Each speaks their own language and responds to different types of stimuli. Before hiring a lobbyist, extensive research should be done and references should be reviewed. Funds must be an amalgam of city, state, and federal funding combined with contributions from foundations, corporations, individuals, friends, and grassroots supporters.

Both the state and federal governments may be easier to approach once city funding is achieved. With respect to the state and federal agencies, it's important to research what problems they are currently focusing on, as this will help you streamline your efforts in those specific directions to better your chances.

Getting to know your local congresspeople is critical. By putting your agency on their radar and being clear about what you are hoping to accomplish, you will position yourself in a prime spot for receiving government support.

## FOUNDATIONS

Foundations are the primary source that most not-for-profits start with, and that is because every foundation has a purpose and a commitment to fund certain areas of social distress that are in dire need of services. You can determine which foundations are committed to which social issues through organizations such as the Foundation Center. Simply by inserting your dedicated social problem on their website or by visiting their library, you will quickly be able to determine which foundations you should pursue for your agency.

It will be helpful to research what foundations fund not-for-profits that are similar to the one you're starting. For example, since my focus was going to be criminal justice reform, those were the types of agencies that I would be looking at. This can be determined by using the annual reports of these comparable agencies to discover what aspect of their operations were funded by specific foundations who were willing to support them.

Focus on Google and social media platforms to compile a list of foundations interested in your issue. Wealthy individuals are also a very important resource for the funding of agencies. Many have family foundations through which they fund nonprofits, and that information is available through their websites or the all-important Foundation Center, which will also specifically note the needs and problems our society is facing.

The names of other foundations to be pursued can come from your board of directors. Hopefully in the recruiting process for potential board members, they were asked if they were connected with foundation board members who would be interested in funding your agency.

Board members who have homes suitable for entertaining and holding intimate gatherings are another way of raising significant funds. This is a great option for individually hosted events as well as celebrating important events where clients would be able to meet and greet potential funders. Another opportunity for raising funds is through the use of an annual benefit where interested parties can reach out to friends and widen the number of potential supporters. In order to raise the profile of GOSO, I would often attempt to get celebrities to speak. One of GOSO's speaking success stories was NYC District Attorney Cyrus Vance Jr.

While it might sound strange to have a DA speak at a benefit for the formerly incarcerated, we wanted both our members and support-ers to understand that we supported law and order in our society and had great relationships with both the DA's office and the NYPD. This did not conflict with our desire to have the criminal justice system reformed and be more just by being less focused on our clients.

At the same time that you are researching possible funding sources, you should be putting together proposals to potential funders. There is a basic format to be followed; however, I would recommend that you find a unique way to set yourself apart from competition.

Determine what aspect of your nonprofit sets you apart, and make that the focus of your proposal.

GOSO's unique angle stemmed from the fact that I was a corporate executive on a mission to transfer my business skills and experiences to the nonprofit world, and my focus leaned heavily on the theme of a return on investment (ROI). I am quite sure it may have been the first time that a foundation board had the concept of an ROI put before them as the reason to support a brand-new not-for-profit agency.

No two applications are exactly alike, since no two foundations will have the exact same mission and require the same type of information. Below, I have put together a generic agenda that would have to be amended to adhere to the specific requests that every potential funder will invariably have. At the same time, it is imperative that the requesting agency feature their unique talents that make them logical recipients of their requested funding. They should be emphasizing any competitive advantages that they possess to ensure that their request has the best possible chance of being selected for funding in a highly competitive market.

The best location for these types of meetings is in your own office because that will give the prospective foundation the opportunity to see your agency in operation and meet your staff. More importantly, it will allow your clients to participate in your presentation. Foundations appreciate having the opportunity to meet those who are benefitting from the funding that they are considering providing.

## FORMAT FOR LIVE OR WRITTEN FUNDING REQUESTS

- Mission and purpose
- Agency history and programs

- Population served

- What distinguishes your agency from other similar programs

- Outcomes to be achieved by this proposal

- Strategy to execute your plan

- Financial details

- Timing

If you want to increase your chances of getting funding, it's critical to frequently attend benefits for other similar agencies. This will allow you to get on the circuit and meet and greet funders who are already donating to comparable causes.

As part of this process, you will meet other social agency leaders who can counsel you on the inside workings of certain foundations as well as the city and state governments where you offer services.

Being out there so that you are seen and heard in the right network of influencers in your city of residence will do wonders for the success of your agency. Having a solid reputation within the community will help you be well received by potential future funders.

# CHAPTER ELEVEN

# Staffing

*It's not the size of the dog in the fight, it's the size of the fight in the dog.*
**—MARK TWAIN**

It is extremely difficult to have sufficient funding to fully staff a new not-for-profit at its onset, which is why you must be prepared to be incredibly busy. But keep in mind ... it's all for a good cause, and with a solid work ethic and proper preparation, you will be successful.

When I started GOSO, I also made sure that newly hired employees were aware that they would be wearing many hats at first, and that once we could afford to hire fully trained managers, some of their functions would be relinquished. As its founder, I learned that lesson from the day that I decided to create GOSO. I opened up shop in the morning and closed in the evening, I answered phones, handled mail, met with clients, made the necessary trips to Rikers Island. Needless to say, I was a very, very busy man.

The good thing about being the one responsible for all those functions was that I knew exactly how to train my newly hired employees when they took over these tasks.

I made it clear that every new hire had to have the ability to multitask and follow a strict modus operandi in their area of expertise. Having this combination of traits helped GOSO employees thrive.

As new people were hired and they took on multiple tasks, they were then able to do exactly the same as I had done, learning it all from the ground up. In a sense, every one of us was a social entrepreneur in our own right.

As discussed previously, every new employee had to understand that GOSO was going to be all about the guys, and they were going to be asked to put their own personal needs on the back burner in deference to the guys. Most importantly, they had to know that every expense request had to bring added value to the program.

The core group of GOSO employees who would be working with the GOSO guys were required to have a master's degree in social work (MSW). Every reentry organization that I looked at as a reference point hired caseworkers, but they did not mandate that their employees had to have a master's degree in the field from a reputable school of social work. This decision was a costly one in that the MSW's compensation was much higher than the caseworkers'; however, it was a cost that paid great dividends to young GOSO guys who needed that professional guidance.

Over 60 percent of the young men on Rikers Island had mental health issues, which was why having qualified, licensed social workers on staff was a necessity. In more serious cases, we were going to have psychiatrists available on retainer to work with the young men.

I felt that the third *E* (emotional well-being) had to be professionally addressed, or the first two (education and employment) did not have a chance of succeeding. And since my strength was in employment, and I was adding an educational unit funded by the city, it was imperative that the emotional well-being segment be filled with strong leadership.

I was very fortunate in the hiring of our first director of social services. Paul was passionate about our mission; he hired extremely well and was an excellent supervisor. He was like a son to me in that our styles mirrored each other. He stayed at GOSO for six years, and when he resigned to take up an acting and teaching role, I knew that I was going to have a difficult time finding someone to step into his shoes.

Once again, the difference between the for-profit and not-for-profit worlds became apparent to me.

As an entrepreneur I could make personnel decisions independently, and I didn't have to take into consideration pay scales, relationships between different employees, and the politics. In the non-profit world salaries are all structured, which made it more difficult for me to offer him a much higher salary in an effort to keep him.

Most importantly, in the early stages of a not-for-profit such as GOSO, with funding not readily available, each employee is asked to do considerably more than in an older, more established organization. This was necessary from the get-go since we were going to be asked to produce the same reports as larger agencies if we were going to qualify for funding.

Then there were the young men who we were going to be working with, who needed services provided to them in a timely fashion once they were released from incarceration. The fact that we were a brand-new organization did not give us a free pass to lag behind in providing the much-needed services in a timely fashion.

The main difference between staffing a for-profit versus a not-for-profit organization is tied to the very basic difference in their missions. An organization driven by the not-for-profit motive is created to make a difference in people's lives, and their employees are required to focus on their clients and their needs versus the bottom-line focus of the for-profit employees.

Over the sixteen years that I ran GOSO, my biggest employee issues came from the fact that the managers, in addition to focusing on the needs of their clients, were also required to take into consideration the financial needs of the organization.

> **An organization driven by the not-for-profit motive is created to make a difference in people's lives, and their employees are required to focus on their clients and their needs versus the bottom-line focus of the for-profit employees.**

This was particularly important to me since I had founded and built GOSO on a business model with strict management and financial controls that I knew would impress both government and private funding resources. That philosophy was a key ingredient in every funding request. It paid off by having impressive donations from responsive and generous funders. At the same time, GOSO's guarantee that every funder would be rewarded with a return on their investment was a promise that accompanied our acceptance of funding from every resource.

We were particularly good at presenting GOSO to potential funding sources because I made sure that every presentation featured a team approach to our program. Yes, I was the founder and the spiritual leader of the organization; but I had put together a staff that was professional, hardworking, and most importantly, responsive to our clients' needs. There was an accountability that I had instilled in the staff that was also very apparent when they spoke about their role in the organization. It was my responsibility as their leader to teach, train, and inspire them in their development as professionals. They responded by being loyal, hardworking staff members who cared about each other and, most importantly, our guys. Finally, having GOSO guys talk about their experiences both while incarcerated as well as when they were released delivered a powerful message to potential funders.

Over the years I always knew which of the staff was giving their all, and I did my best to reward them for their efforts, although not as much as I would have liked to. On the subject of giving their all, I was always on the search for employees who not only performed their duties but went well over and above their responsibilities.

Throughout my life as a social entrepreneur and a corporate leader, I have always lived by the following adage: If you have an important task to be done, give it to the busiest person.

The rationale behind this motto is that the busiest person is always the first one done while having done the most complete job. The reason you don't give that task to someone with time on their hands is that they have time on their hands because they were not really working hard enough to finish their tasks.

The administrative hiring is very similar to the corporate world because those employees are tasked with supporting the professional staff just as they are in the business world. I also quickly learned the importance of hiring a volunteer director as well as a head of publicity who would be managing our messaging to potential funders. In addition to these unique and essential roles, I hired a publicity person to manage the outside suppliers. Like most things in the early days of GOSO, this was handled on a consultancy basis since it was more efficient than having full-time employees.

Until you can afford to hire staff in a not-for-profit organization, it's important to keep in mind the fact that you will be doing a lot of the work yourself at first.

# CHAPTER TWELVE
# Finance and Legal Services

*During your life, never stop dreaming. No one can take away*
*your dreams. Our future is our confidence and self-esteem.*
—**TUPAC SHAKUR**

## FINANCE

Not-for-profit financial affairs need to be maintained by a strong financial officer and maintained accurately. Monthly, quarterly, and annual financial records need to be documented, quarterly reports should be presented to the board of directors, and all division heads should be part of the process. This helps everyone gauge how the agency is performing. From a regulatory point of view, an annual audit with all funding sources must be completed in a professional manner and demonstrate excellent results. An outside accounting firm and auditing firm should be put on retainer to accomplish these tasks.

Coming off my entrepreneurial experience, I already had a relationship with an excellent accounting firm whom I interviewed for the accounting role at GOSO. I learned that they also had not-for-profit experience, and they connected me with an auditing firm that also had not-for-profit experience, so I was set immediately on this aspect of our organization.

Coming from the corporate world, I was going to insist on the tightest possible financial controls. That started with making sure that every single employee was able to produce a rationale for and understand the ramifications of their financial decisions. Too often in the not-for-profit world, I had heard that executives in the field were overly concerned, and rightly so, with their clients' needs. However, I made it clear when every employee was hired that they would need to pay strict attention to all of their efforts that had a financial ramification. I had every intention of spending whatever was necessary to support our clients; however, the concept of added value was part of their basic training at GOSO. We needed our clients to take responsibility for their actions. At the same time, we wanted to make sure that we were adding real value to their lives.

Projects of any size required a process that necessitated at least three bids, and budgetary limits were set for each employee. I made the final decisions and had to sign off on any purchase over one hundred dollars. There were only two credit cards, and they were both in my name and GOSO's.

In the corporate world, I had always been a tough but fair negotiator, and with a limited budget in the not-for-profit world, I had to be an even tougher negotiator. I was not opposed to using the purpose of GOSO as a way to drive prices down. In other words, I would let potential suppliers know of GOSO's mission and the importance of our service to society. We were not trying to get an unfair inside price but rather one where we ask them if they had "sharpened their pencils" and were giving us the best possible price for their services based on what we were doing for society.

The head of any not-for-profit must be a fierce advocate for his/her agency at all times. That advocacy must be part of any business negotiation, talks with government officials, and part of virtually every public statement that is made. You will be advocating in a world where funders whom you approach are also constantly being bombarded for funding by other not-for-profits. Why should they pick your agency for funding as opposed to other agencies whose missions are similar to yours?

**You will be advocating in a world where funders whom you approach are also constantly being bombarded for funding by other not-for-profits. Why should they pick your agency for funding as opposed to other agencies whose missions are similar to yours?**

Furthermore, all suppliers had to produce at least three references supporting their claims of performance. We had very good relationships with all of our suppliers because we were tough negotiators, but we were fair and very loyal customers. We had that kind of reputation, and therefore we always had the best suppliers in the city who really wanted our business.

What they liked best about us was that we paid our bills on time, and in the event that we were going to have a late payment, we would be sure to let them know prior to the due date of the invoice. There is nothing that a supplier likes better than being paid on time, and if a payment is going to be late, they appreciate being advised so they can monitor their payables accordingly. During my time in running GOSO, we did not have a single financial dispute that wasn't settled amicably.

## LEGAL SUPPORT

Because GOSO would be working with clients who came from dire circumstances, it was critical that we had strong legal advice at all times, especially when it came to the actions that my staff would be facing. It helped that my son is a lawyer and counseled me on legal matters on a pro bono basis regarding several disputes.

Having lawyers on staff is expensive and not necessary; however, from day one, a legal firm should be put on retainer to ensure your nonprofit is protected legally at all times. There should be consistent open lines of communication so that if the organization is served with any type of legal action, the law firm is able to respond in a timely fashion. I kept that function solely in my hands during my entire time running GOSO.

Tight, documented communication would have to be maintained at all times by every employee. In the world of nonprofits, with lives on the line, the possibility of failure is omnipresent due to the dire circumstances in which our clients found themselves in. In addition, mental health challenges were always a concern. There would be difficult decisions that needed to be made to ensure the clients' needs were being attended to. Needless to say, the clients' needs came first; however, it was paramount that the agency wasn't in any conflict with solid legal grounds when it came to protecting the clients.

Here again, the difference between for-profit and not-for-profit work was huge. In the corporate world, we were dealing with numbers and hopefully profits. In the nonprofit world, lives were at stake. Since we were going to be working in and around the criminal justice system, it was imperative that our social workers understood that lives were at stake based on every decision they would be making in support of their clients, and those decisions would always be subject to legal review should any lawsuits be brought against the agency.

# CHAPTER THIRTEEN

# Public Relations, Lobbying, and Marketing

*The road to success is not easy to navigate, but with hard work, drive, and passion, it's possible to achieve the American dream.*
**—TOMMY HILFIGER**

Since my corporate resume included public relations, marketing, and lobbying, it wasn't necessary to hire salaried staff members for these services. I knew that each of them required full-time attention that might best be handled by using experienced service providers on a consultancy basis. I felt comfortable in my ability to find the right companies to represent GOSO in all of these important aspects of our strategic planning. I needed to find a publicity, marketing, and public relations company staffed by professionals who were personable, likeable, and articulate networkers who, most importantly, had extensive nonprofit experience. Since they would be the face of the agency, their ability to deliver impressive, convincing messages on a moment's notice would be critical.

These consultants had an advantage because they would be guided by my knowledge and expertise. I had the talent to sell GOSO simply because of my background and the fact that I had created the organization. Telling the story to the press and broadcast media came naturally to me, and my years in the corporate world had prepared me to do it for a cause other than making money.

I may not be the best writer in the world, but put me in front of a camera, and what you will get is the consummate salesperson. I know how to convince people to buy into a proposition. I started with a great story, since GOSO was a new reentry agency that was already setting records when it came to reducing recidivism for young men mostly of color and ages sixteen to twenty-four. Numbers don't lie, and GOSO had a reduction from over 60 percent to under 15 percent. How did we get publicity from the very beginning? We were blessed by having criminal justice reform become a hot media story, and I took advantage of that by telling our story firsthand.

It was the story of a corporate executive turned social entrepreneur who took his Principal for a Day gig and founded Getting Out and Staying Out. He then hired some extraordinary people along the way, and together they turned it into one of the most successful reentry programs in New York City's history.

I took the story as far as I could on my own but then recognized that it was time for me to find a lobbyist/public relations firm to capitalize on what I had already accomplished by taking the story to even broader-based media. The goal was to put GOSO on the radar screen of the New York City governing bodies that were funding criminal justice reform at the time.

Needless to say, it was critical that I found someone who firmly believed in the agency's message and had a passion for getting that story out effectively. Being able to take a simple story and transform it into a spectacular moment that spotlighted GOSO on a consistent basis was essential for the agency to make progress.

Marketing is marketing, whether you are in the for-profit or not-for-profit world. Marketers are responsible for creating the agency's message and presenting it to a target audience determined by in-depth research. This process is completed to ensure that the specified audience will act according to the message.

**Marketing is marketing, whether you are in the for-profit or not-for-profit world.**

It is critical that the marketing team coordinates an annual plan to deliver the agency's message via print, social media, and broadcast media in a consistent way.

One of the biggest differences between for-profit and not-for-profit organizations is in the public policy arena. While corporations do not primarily get involved in public policy, not-for-profits work tirelessly to help set public policies that directly affect their organizations.

The messages that need to be delivered specifically to government agencies and public officials have to be fully coordinated and presented in a timely fashion. The marketing team must conduct an analysis of the critical positions of power in these agencies so they can determine where to direct the proposals that are worthy of funding.

As part of the marketing process, it's essential to nurture government and community relationships in an efficient and professional manner. This will ultimately position the not-for-profit in a place where their funding requests will be granted year after year, much in the same way GOSO succeeded.

A lobbyist should be hired on a consultant basis, and the choice is determined by conducting an extensive search that reviews credentials and includes reference checks. The most important aspect of the search is to determine how effective their clients have been in achieving government contracts on the city and state levels. Knowing the account executive responsible for your account is key; however, it's important to keep in mind that an agency's success doesn't always mean that the right person will be assigned to your account. The leaders of your agency's lobbyist team must also be involved in telling the agency's story with passion in a competitive marketplace. I believe strongly in top-to-top meetings.

Your marketing team should be able to secure government funding, press coverage for the voice of the agency, interviews, and potential opportunities that are in line with your mission. It will be the not-for-profit's responsibility to provide the lobbyist with the ammunition for the marketing/media plan, which will hopefully support the funding requests on a city and state level.

When I was tasked with acquiring consultants for marketing purposes, I had no doubt that GOSO would be able to deliver and provide the impressive measurements and outcomes for the lobbyists to use successfully with potential funders.

It had to be a team effort, captained by yours truly, but also involving staff members who had the gift of being able to talk on their feet with the same passion that I brought to every opportunity to sell GOSO.

I had much to accomplish. I was already sixty-eight years old when I started GOSO, and I had a lot to achieve in the next fifteen years, at which time I would probably retire and turn it over to the next generation. The good news was that my plan was executed right on schedule.

*My first day at Riker's Island.*

*My appearance at the White House.*

*Carlos Palanco graduates college.*

*The GOSO guys.*

*The GOSO guys.*

*Muhammad Ali, the GOAT (greatest of all time).*

*Tribute letter from staff.*

Mayor Michael R. Bloomberg Hosts Barbeque in Honor of New York City
Boards and Commissions
Gracie Mansion, Manhattan
July 21, 2004

*Picture with Mayor Bloomberg.*

THE CITY OF NEW YORK
OFFICE OF THE MAYOR
NEW YORK, NY 10007

March 30, 2007

To Whom It May Concern:

Mark Goldsmith is having a significant impact on one of society's most vexing problems and deepest disgraces -- the staggering number of young men of color doomed to a lifetime of educational neglect, poverty, and incarceration.

Mark gives a damn about the lives of these young people. And they respond incredibly well to his mentoring and life-coaching. To say that his approach has been innovative and successful is a profound understatement. The impact has been nothing short of miraculous: while two out of three young men released from jail typically will be re-incarcerated within a year, only a handful of young men who've been through Mark's program have been rearrested.

The Mayor was so impressed with Mark's results, that he allocated funding in next year's budget to double the size of the program and to study its impact. Mark's work has provoked a new level of policy dialogue within City government.

Mark is one of the most effective people I know. His entrepreneurial spirit and CEO personality make people want to follow him. When I first met him during a site visit to Rikers Island to review the jail's educational programs, I saw how his passion for helping young inmates to turn their lives around motivated and inspired others around him. And in the year and a half since, I've seen him expand his organization to include a cadre of volunteers from the business world and mainstream society.

Be they teenagers, prison guards, educators, or other older adults from the business world, Mark's no-nonsense, results-oriented approach resonates with people. And he brings compassion and a love of humanity to his work that you can feel as soon as you walk into his East Harlem office. We all have that within us; but, Mark has been uniquely successful in channeling it into his new work.

The wonderful thing about Mark is that he actually has potential to achieve even more in transforming lives and breaking the cycle of incarceration and poverty. It is only a question of resources and time.

I can't think of anyone who would deserve the Purpose Prize more than Mark Goldsmith and I am pleased to offer you my enthusiastic and unqualified recommendation.

Sincerely,

Anthony Tassi
Director, Adult Education

*Testimonial from Anthony Tassi.*

# THE WALL STREET JOURNAL.

DOWJONES. · · · · ·   MONDAY, MARCH 17, 2008 · VOL. CCLI NO. 63   ★ ★ ★ ★ $1.

Last week: DJIA 11951.09 ▲ 57.40 0.5%   NASDAQ 2212.49 unch   NIKKEI 12241.60 ▼ 4.2%   DJ STOXX 50 3017.31 ▼ 1.3%   10-YR TREASURY ▲ 1.00, yield 3.423%   OIL $110.21 ▲ $5.06   EURO $1.5671   YEN 99.32

**IN THE LEAD | By Carol Hymowitz**

## Executives Teach Inmates How to Be Employees

Mark Goldsmith didn't expect to go to jail when he volunteered to be "principal for a day" at a New York City school. But after requesting a "tough school," he was assigned to Horizon Academy, a high school for inmates ages 18 to 24 at Rikers Island prison.

Mr. Goldsmith, a former executive at Revlon and Shiseido, was ushered through locked gates to the prison's classroom. Standing in front of his new class, he looked at the young students and saw

"I started at the bottom, got in earlier than anyone and left later, and then I got promoted—and you can do this, too," he explained to the class.

Mr. Goldsmith felt the teaching experience was rewarding for both sides and volunteered again for the program. After, he decided he needed more than just one day a year with these inmates if he were to help them turn their lives around. In 2005, he launched his own nonprofit, Getting Out and Staying Out. GOSO, as it is called, now is working with 275 inmates

with have been arrested again since the group was formed three years ago. That figure compares with two-thirds of prisoners released annually nationwide who have been rearrested, according to the U.S. Department of Justice.

In addition, three-quarters of the former prisoners counseled by GOSO, which receives private and public funding, are employed or attending school.

As former business executives, Mr. Goldsmith and other GOSO volunteers offer something else that's different: They understand who gets hired and promoted in a variety of industries and can teach inmates how to turn the entry-level jobs they typically get after prison into a career.

"A lot of programs for prisoners are run by former prisoners or social workers, but Mark brings a business perspective, he's a role model of success and he tells kids who have never thought they can be successful that they're entitled to that," says Anthony Tassi, executive director of adult education in the mayor's office, New York.

GOSO also urges participants to keep returning for counseling so they can keep advancing.

"GOSO is successful because unlike other groups it works with young prisoners to plan for re-entry from the day they're incarcerated, and then sticks with them over the long term," says Hazel Beckles, head of the planned re-entry for incarcerated adolescents program at Community Service Society of New York, a nonprofit organization.

Mr. Goldsmith and Richard Block, the retired CEO of a 2,000-employee entertainment-packaging company, spend several days a week at Rikers, counseling inmates studying for their high-school equivalency diplomas. The pair believe that the same motivation principles—including perseverance and adventure—
*Please turn to page B3*

Mark Goldsmith finds long-term job counseling is key to helping turn around prisoners' lives.

in them signs of his own difficult youth. He had never committed a crime; but he told the students he thought he was dumb, and graduated near the bottom of his high-school class. He enrolled in college at night because his wife insisted, but he didn't think he could achieve anything. Then, he landed his first business job at 29 at Coty, a fragrance company then owned by Pfizer, and proved his hard work could earn him advances.

serving sentences in upstate New York prisons and 150 at Rikers.

Mr. Goldsmith and 14 other current or retired executives who volunteer at GOSO, based in Harlem, plus a paid staff of six, are working to counter the familiar story of prisoners getting released without skills, jobs, money or a place to live, and then resorting to crime only to get locked up again. Fewer than 10% of the 400 released inmates GOSO has worked

## Executives Counsel Inmates on How to Advance in the Workplace

Continued from page B1

some ambition—that they used to help their employees build a career can help young prisoners.

On a recent morning, the two men gathered with 10 inmates in a classroom watched closely by prison guards.

"What's going to be hardest for you when you get out of here?" asked Mr. Goldsmith.

"Staying away from the friends I got into trouble with—and getting a job," one inmate quickly answered.

The group fell silent, though, when asked what jobs they wanted after prison. "What are you good at, what do you like to do?" insisted Mr. Block.

One inmate blurted that he had taught his cousin how to play basketball and might like to be a school basketball coach. Another said he loved to cook. "We have three GOSO members who are now in culinary school," said Mr. Block, who promised to bring him restaurant menus on his next visit to Rikers.

Because GOSO works only with young prisoners who are attending

school, and haven't been in prison long, it has a better chance of success, acknowledges Mr. Goldsmith. Even this select group, however, faces steep hurdles after release—from steering clear of gangs, to avoiding drugs, to following strict parole rules and to mending relationships with relatives.

GOSO members are urged to come to the group's office within a week of their release. They are each given an alarm clock, mass-transit cards for commuting, a subway map and a calendar to keep track of appointments.

Roberto Moran, GOSO's career-development manager, provides individual job and education coaching. The group maintains a job bank of openings with employers willing to hire former prisoners, gives out college and other education scholarships and holds seminars. A retired construction-industry executive, for instance, teaches what is required to become a skilled tradesperson.

Mr. Goldsmith tells everyone who gets a job interview that "the three most important things to say are, 'I'm

never late, I work very hard. I never get sick.' " He warns them to dress in conservative clothes, avoid faddish hairstyles and to remember to turn off their cellphones for the interview.

He encouraged Larry, who spent eight months at Rikers before the robbery charge against him was dropped, to talk directly to the hiring manager when he applied for a job at Target. When Larry wasn't selected from a crowd of other applicants, he stuck around until the manager noticed him and invited him to his office. Within an hour, he had a job.

"I got lucky," he told Mr. Goldsmith. "You made your luck," Mr. Goldsmith replied.

Not everyone sticks with the program. "There are disappointments," says Mr. Block. He says he felt most let down when a Rikers inmate he'd spent hours mentoring and loaned money to never came to GOSO's office after his release.

But those who do show up say GOSO is a "home" they can keep returning to for help. Some former inmates drop by

just to chat or to share good news about a job, or talk about a problem they are having with their mother, girlfriend or boss. Many call the office daily, or bring by their relatives. Others return for counseling whenever they lose or don't land a job, want a different one, or decide to go back to school.

"I know it's up to me to change, but GOSO always receives me like family and helped me change my life," says Mark, who was in and out of prison three times between the ages of 16 and 23 on drug dealing and robbery convictions. He met Mr. Block at Rikers when the former executive held a workshop on how to write a business plan for a small company.

Now 25 and off parole, he worked at the delicatessen counter of a supermarket when released 12 months ago, but he was fired when he threw out some turkey he hadn't sliced properly. He talked to Mr. Block, who told him, "don't bury your mistakes, it's all right to make some."

Now he has a job driving patients to and from hospital appointments. Last week, when he passed the test required

to drive a van with 40 passengers, he immediately called Mr. Block.

When Mr. Block first volunteered at GOSO nearly three years ago, Mr. Goldsmith told him that if he felt ambivalent about helping people convicted of crimes, he shouldn't get involved. He has turned away other executives who were afraid to use their real names with inmates. Some of his friends tell him he's crazy to spend so much time with convicts.

"If they'd get to know some of these kids better, they'd know they're not hopeless, he says. "A lot of them are as smart and talented as anyone you meet in business, they just haven't had anyone to help them."

*Article in* The Wall Street Journal.

50¢

NEW YORK CITY

# Newsday

WWW.NYNEWSDAY.COM      WEDNESDAY, JUNE 23, 2004 | CITY EDITION

# These inmates hold keys

COMMENTARY
**ELLIS HENICAN**

"I told her on Thursday," Manuel Mena was saying on Rikers Island. "I said, 'Ma, I'm graduating high school. You can come and see it if you want to.'"

The mother did not need to be invited twice. A train ride to a bus ride to a wait for clearance at the guard station to a full-body visitor's search. What did that mean to a mother whose troublesome 20-year-old son would be getting his high-school diploma?

"I had to come," said the mother, whose name is Sonia Mena.

And so yesterday, mother and son — along with Manuel's wife, Lynette Ramirez, and their 2-year-old son, Andrew — were huddled with dozens of other smiling young men and their loved ones in a steamy jail gymnasium that was decorated with balloons and streamers and colorful signs. But the party decorations were no match at all for the brightness of a mother's eyes as she gazed — and just kept gazing — at her tall, lanky son in his blue cap and gown.

"He looks good," the mother said.

"High school graduate," the wife agreed, as little Andrew crawled nearby on the gymnasium floor.

For a moment at least, even Manuel Mena put aside the studied nonchalance of the jailhouse and agreed that, whatever he might or might not be responsible for on the outside, he had actually accomplished something in here.

"I went to Stevenson High School" in the Bronx, he said, before being arrested on a second-degree murder charge. "I figured that was probably the end of school for me."

But it wasn't.

Once at Rikers, he found his

NEWSDAY PHOTO / AUDREY C. TIERNAN

Horizon Academy graduate Manuel Mena is one proud papa yesterday with his son, Andrew, on Rikers Island.

way to Horizon Academy, a joint project of the city's Education and Correction departments.

The school opened six years ago under a federal-court order in a lawsuit brought by Legal Aid. The judge ruled that, even behind bars, young people have a right to attend school. Exactly what that means is still a subject of intense legal wrangling. But Gloria Ortiz, Horizon's tireless principal, wasn't the type to just sit around and wait while the courts try to decide what school is.

"A high school should have a graduation," she said as her students took their places in the gym. "We were never able to have a graduation before. This is our first. The achievement of these students is one of the positive things happening on Rikers Island. It should be celebrated the way graduations are celebrated everywhere."

So the principal reserved the gym at Rikers' George Motchan Detention Center. She collected 32 caps and gowns. She rounded up a commencement speaker, who was me. She got permission for correction officers to escort the graduating students from Horizon's four separate Rikers sites.

Invitations went out to the relatives. Some of the teachers stayed late on Monday to decorate the gym. Several of the graduates agreed to speak.

And damned if they didn't have a high school graduation

on Rikers Island yesterday!

It wasn't so different, really, from the high school graduations being held all over New York at this time of the year, except there was no prom and the students had to go back to their dorms when the festivities were done.

Several teachers spoke, as did some officials from the city Correction and Education departments.

Mark Goldsmith, a retired cosmetics executive who is a volunteer mentor to Horizon students, reminded everyone why programs like Horizon matter so much. "Two out of three guys that come to Rikers Island come back to Rikers Island," he told the graduates. "This must stop."

The only answer, Goldsmith said, is preparing these students — in practical and psychological ways — for the free lives that, sooner or later, almost all of them will return to.

In my talk, I tried to walk a line between celebration and inspiration.

The students were certainly not shy about expressing themselves. Every last one of them thanked special teachers and attentive family members.

"I am proud to be a graduate of this school," Corey Branch said to his fellow graduates from the podium. "When I walk beyond these gates again, I will do so proudly as a learned man."

"When I was out in the world before," graduate Morris Evans said, "I was mentally enslaved and physically free. It took me being here, physically enslaved, to become mentally free."

But it was one of the teachers, Penny La Forest, who put the day's message in the most practical terms. This year's graduation, she said, is only a start.

"More rooms, more books, more money, more teachers, so we can graduate more students," she said. "Really, isn't that what corrections is all about?"

---

*Article in* Newsday.

**DAILY ⊡ NEWS**

$1.00   www.nydailynews.com   **NEW YORK'S HOMETOWN NEWSPAPER**   Sunday, January 25, 2004

**LENDING A HAND** Mark Goldsmith (r.), president of Getting Out and Staying Out, has mentored about 250 Rikers inmates,

SUSANA BATES

# School of hard knocks

## He teaches Rikers inmates to get out & stay out

By NICOLE BODE
DAILY NEWS STAFF WRITER

Mark Goldsmith faced the row of Rikers Island inmates and raised one of the most crucial questions of their incarcerated lives.

"What percentage of the guys in Rikers do you think come back?" Goldsmith asked his five-man audience, all between the ages of 18 and 21. "Seventy percent. That means three of you guys are coming back here once you get out — and what I can do to help you," continued Goldsmith, a Manhattan businessman and founder of the nonprofit prison-transition program Getting Out and Staying Out.

Goldsmith thought up the program last year after being paired up with Manhattan-based lawyer Marvin Schechter as principal-for-a-day at Horizon Academy, Rikers' high school for 18 to 21 year olds.

"I said to Marvin, 'You're talking to them about getting out of here, and I'm talking to them about staying out of

here,'" Goldsmith said. "So I got all excited and went right out and patented the name."

Goldsmith, who worked in the cosmetics industry for decades and now heads a business consulting agency, said he was troubled by the rising jail population, and the dwindling city budget available for transition services.

So he decided to tap into the power of the private sector. After applying for nonprofit status and obtaining clearance from the departments of Correction and Education, Goldsmith launched the program through Horizon Academy eight months ago.

He now spends about two days a week at Rikers, lecturing and mentoring small groups of students from 9 a.m. to 2 p.m. on everything from legal rights to career opportunities to life skills. In October, he coordinated a visit from hip-hop mogul Russell Simmons and his brother the Rev. Run, from Run DMC.

"You can tell he's really trying to help us," said 19-year-old Abdul Khan of Coney Island. "Hopefully, when I go home, I'm going to be working with him, too. I hope I don't go get in the same predicament that I'm in right now and I don't

come back."

In addition, Goldsmith works with inmates who have recently been released, coaching them on how to utilize the time they spent in prison and how to manage once they get out.

About 250 inmates have gone through the program so far, including seven ex-offenders who are now being mentored outside of jail. Goldsmith hopes eventually to double that number — capping it at about a quarter of the 2,000 inmates who pass through Horizon Academy each year. He is in the process of applying for private funding and hopes to secure a Harlem office and hire staffers by the end of the year.

None of the ex-offenders he has worked with has returned to jail. One of his success stories is a young man who was released over the summer and is currently working as a film editor.

Goldsmith has met with him three times since his release — using a midtown Starbucks for their interim office.

> *"There aren't a lot of organizations in the community that welcome these guys with open arms."*
>
> TIM LISANTE

"It is imperative that I stick with him during the first few months of his being released, as this is the time period that he is most likely to revert to previous behavior," Goldsmith said.

The program improves upon existing transitional services because it is one of the first to follow inmates from incarceration to freedom, officials said.

"As you can probably imagine, there aren't a lot of organizations in the community that welcome these guys with open arms," said Tim Lisante, the Department of Education local instructional superintendent in charge of Rikers Island schools. "But if they don't get reconnected to the community, then we were not as effective as we wanted to be."

Lisante said that the Ed Department would ultimately like to see Goldsmith's program expand into other prison-based school systems across the city.

"We could use this type of program in every borough," he said

*Article in* Daily News.

122

*Entrance to Rikers Island.*

*Founder and Principal of Horizon Academy
on Rikers Island Gloria Ortiz.*

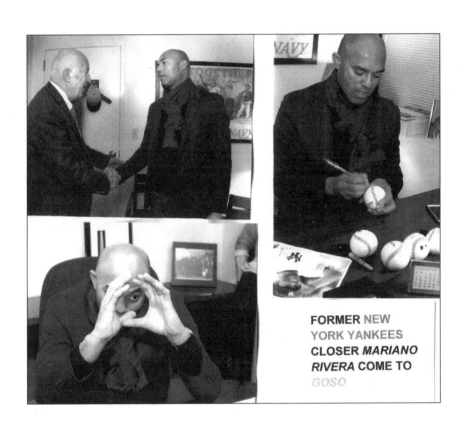

FORMER NEW
YORK YANKEES
CLOSER *MARIANO
RIVERA* COME TO
GOSO

*Mariano Rivera visits GOSO.*

# CHAPTER FOURTEEN

# Measurement and Outcomes

*All I'm trying to do is survive and make good out of the
dirty, nasty, unbelievable lifestyle that they gave me.*
—**TUPAC SHAKUR**

Coming from the business world, where I knew that my compensation was based primarily on the numbers, delivering the bottom line was key. I was a Milton Friedman corporate executive trained to deliver the bottom line or be ready to be replaced if I didn't.

From the onset I realized that once I started a nonprofit, delivering results would be my agency's strong point, just as it was in my corporate life. I focused on my unique business education and background in public speaking and used this to my advantage when I presented to foundations as well as government agencies to emphasize how strongly I felt about results and outcomes. For the most part, none of them had ever heard from a social entrepreneur who wasn't trained and educated in social services. This made me different, and I used that uniqueness to my advantage.

In the not-for-profit world, many agencies are so consumed by the curing of social problems that they neglect the numbers side of the business, and that is a big mistake. After all, any funder is entitled to see the specific results of their funding, not rough estimates. Results are going to encourage them to either start funding your agency and/ or continue funding you once you are on their books.

When it comes to establishing the measurements and outcomes, the entire staff must be involved so they become just as committed to them as the founder and leaders are. All staff members should be included in developing and monitoring measurements and outcomes over the time period of any particular grant.

The measurements should be both substantial and realistic. Then, needless to say, the outcomes (results) must be accurately documented even if they are less than promised. This is not an easy report to do, should the outcomes fall short of what had been promised to the funder.

The entire staff must be involved in this process, even though the work they do might not be directly involved in specific number development. It's important that all employees have a clear under-standing of the inner workings of the agency and how performance is being evaluated.

Finally, the report should be completed and submitted to funders in an easily understood fashion. The simpler the better. Done well, this will achieve the goal of continued future funding from the entity at hand.

At GOSO, the key measurement was always the recidivism rate. When I first entered the Rikers Island jail, the ongoing recidivism rate for Rikers, as well as the upstate prisons, was always over 60 percent. There was no question in my mind that we could easily beat that number. Little did I know that we would reduce it to under 15 percent once our program was in effect, with our own office where the young men could come for services.

The reasons for our success were very simple. Previously detained young men were getting out of the Rikers Island jail and upstate prisons and returning to the exact same lifestyle and communities that had gotten them incarcerated in the first place. One of the guys once said, "You know what, Mr. G.? When I was released after ten years up top and returned to my neighborhood, I passed the street corner where we used to hang out, and guess what? There they were, the same guys smoking weed and talking the same talk that we were talking over ten years ago when I used to hang out with them. I made a decision that I was never going back to that corner."

What we discussed when they were released, when they were on Rikers Island, and through correspondence when they were in upstate prisons was that if they were going to get a new life when they returned to New York, they could not hang out with the same guys in the same locations. If they did, the same things were going to happen that had caused them to be arrested and incarcerated in the first place.

**When they returned to New York, they could not hang out with the same guys in the same locations. If they did, the same things were going to happen.**

In addition to measuring our reduction in recidivism, equally important, if not more so, were our measurements of educational and employment achievements. Achieving their GED or high school diplomas and moving to community colleges and then four-year colleges or highly technical training were going to set the parameters of their progress in achieving financial independence. Without those diplomas, they wouldn't even be able to apply for better jobs that would provide the types of income that they were looking to achieve.

The other critical measurements that we continued to track were the specific higher levels of success that GOSO guys achieved in the employment arena. Entry-level positions were a given; moving into management and entrepreneurship were the eventual goals.

Once again, on Rikers Island and in our offices, we relayed the correlation of their being the head of a gang or drug cartel and showed them that those same traits could make them successful in the business world. It was the same leadership and passion that they had always had, for the wrong purposes, transformed into legitimate jobs in a world that they'd never even imagined being part of.

To cite an example:

I met Manny on Rikers Island over fifteen years ago. He was sentenced and served over thirteen years in upstate prisons, during which time we corresponded on a regular basis. On his return he got a job making $58,000 at the New York City Health and Hospitals Corporation. He recently called me to report that he had been promoted to a supervisor position, making $62,000 a year. Needless to say, I congratulated him on his achievement and told him we would have lunch shortly to celebrate. I have a picture of him fifteen years ago holding his five-year-old son at his graduation from high school on Rikers Island, where he was valedictorian. His son entered Borough of Manhattan Community College (BMCC) this year as a freshman. In addition to Manny graduating high school on Rikers Island, he earned college degrees while he was incarcerated upstate. He has also volunteered to come and speak with GOSO guys.

What is interesting is that we don't have to follow up with the guys once they start work and become part of the GOSO alumni.

Instead they call on their own to proudly tell us about their latest achievements.

Once again, it's the guys who are producing our measurements and outcomes that we present to foundations and other funding sources, and we show this firsthand by bringing them to presentations to let them tell their stories in person. That is an even better way to present your agency to funders that are interested in hearing your results: "straight from the horse's mouth," as they say.

# CHAPTER FIFTEEN

# Volunteering

*Freedom is never voluntarily given by the oppressor;*
*it must be demanded by the oppressed.*
**—MARTIN LUTHER KING, JR.**

Getting as many committed volunteers as possible has been the secret to success for many not-for-profit organizations. It's important to bring on volunteers who are truly committed to helping vulnerable populations and who show up consistently and do what is necessary to achieve that objective.

First, it is imperative to hire an experienced volunteer director. Enthusiasm for the mission will be paramount, and that person must have the ability to go into venues of all types to spread the word about the great work of the agency. If they don't believe wholeheartedly in your mission and can't passionately talk about it to interested groups, then you have the wrong person. The volunteer director should also be a self-starter, and while they will have staff support, they will essentially operate on their own. Assertiveness and creativity are necessary in this role to ensure that the voice of the agency is heard. Because there is significant competition for volunteers, it's critical that your director has a voice that stands out above others. Part of the volunteer director's job is to motivate the volunteers and keep their interest by having events and programs that give them the feeling that they have joined a great organization with great outcomes. Once they feel that they are contributing to a higher cause than just their own personal needs, they will join.

In addition to having a formidable volunteer director, it is important to offer that person assistance by bringing in high-profile people to volunteer their unique services that can raise awareness of your agency. As mentioned in the board of directors chapter, board member Charles Kushner brought Senator Corey Booker to Rikers Island to meet with the guys, as well as Mariano Rivera, who spent an entire afternoon trying to get the guys to stay focused at all times, just as he did when facing tough batters in the ninth inning.

It is also essential that the agency set the guidelines for any involvement to ensure that there is a clear line between what the staff's responsibilities are and how the volunteers will work with the staff to supplement those efforts and not get in the way of them. Consistency is the most important facet of a volunteer's work, second to the actual work that they do. They must show up on a regular basis, as that dependability is what is missing in the lives of our clients.

From the volunteer's point of view, the not-for-profit world is a unique business to learn because as a volunteer, you do not have to be hired to start getting involved in a particular cause. That opportunity does not exist in the for-profit world, where you must go through the lengthy process of interviewing, intensive screening, and being hired before you can spend one day actually working in a company. While you may generally be carefully screened, it is not as rigorous as a business interview.

The most important work that a potential volunteer must do before getting involved is to first decide what cause they are interested in supporting. There are endless opportunities out there to explore based on your level of interest in a particular social problem. Many of these agencies need all the help they can get.

One never knows what to expect when volunteering to work for a not-for-profit. I made a decision to volunteer to be a Principal for a Day in New York City based on my wife's suggestion, because she felt that I have always been good with young people. And it's only because I asked for the toughest school in New York that they sent me to the notorious Rikers Island, where a high school equivalency program was being run. If I hadn't volunteered to do that, close to ten thousand young men ages sixteen to twenty-four would never have gotten the opportunity to change their lives positively by becoming part of the GOSO program.

**One of the most eye-opening aspects of volunteering is that you never know what might evolve once you decide to make the move to volunteer.**

One of the most eye-opening aspects of volunteering is that you never know what might evolve once you decide to make the move to volunteer. The single most important aspect that I cannot overemphasize enough is that many times you will get even more out of the experience than the people that you are volunteering to help. That is why I am often quoted as saying that it has been my honor to do the work that I have done.

As I was reviewing chapters of this book on Father's Day, once again I was pleasantly surprised to get the following good wishes from John, Manny, and Carlos, all of whose letters are included in chapter six. It is an example of the rewards that you get when you volunteer and make a difference in the world of the people you work with. "Happy Father's Day" from John, who hasn't ever missed thanking me for being there for him for over fifteen years. From Manny: "Mr. G., Happy Father's Day! Hope you enjoy your day alongside your family. Know that you are a father figure to many. God bless you." And from Carlos: "Hope you and Ira are having a pleasant Sunday. Have a blessed day!"

At the same time, you should be thinking about your own personal attributes. What are you good at? What personality traits characterize you and make you appealing to others? Why do people listen to you? Evaluate yourself to determine what makes you feel good about accomplishing difficult tasks.

How you personally like to spend your time is very important, so when you do volunteer, make sure you're doing it for a cause that you love. After all, you do not get paid for volunteer work, and you simply do it because you are committed to making a difference in other people's lives.

Through my daughter I was able to connect with actor and comedian John Leguizamo, who was very anxious to volunteer his services. High-profile people like John are usually very interested in volunteering their time; they just have to be asked.

John really went out of his way by bringing excerpts from two of his one-man off-Broadway hits to Rikers Island. This was no small task. With my significant contacts with the DOC, I was able to get John clearances to bring two shows to Rikers Island. First John spoke with students in their classrooms; then we went into the auditorium where he performed for them. It didn't hurt that close to 40 percent of the young men on Rikers were also Latinx. They could not stop laughing and cheering.

When asked, John then graciously agreed to emcee our annual fundraising benefit, where he went above and beyond and trained some GOSO guys to perform several skits with him. The attendees were blown away by the performances of the guys, and they were amazed by their ability to act. One of the things that became very apparent to me early on is that the guys on Rikers had real creative talent. Little did I know that they were also potential thespians.

As an aside, we also raised more money at that benefit than we had ever raised before, most of it at a silent auction at the end in which John acted as the auctioneer, when he motivated people to bid in amounts never before achieved.

Total costs to GOSO for his two Rikers Island shows followed by his emceeing our benefit—*zero*. This is what volunteering is all about and why it is such an important, unique ingredient in any not-for-profit, perhaps the single most important one of all.

What happens during virtually every volunteer effort is that the volunteers end up getting as much out of the sessions, if not more, than the recipients of the service do. This is the exact same overall reaction that I personally have experienced. GOSO has not only created new lives for our guys; founding GOSO gave me a whole new life of my own, which I'd never thought was possible.

## Scan for GOSO Gala video

## JUNIOR BOARDS

Junior boards are another form of volunteerism. They provide a very important function in that they can be a feeder to the regular board of directors. At the same time, they should have their own agenda, including volunteering at the agency as well as having separate functions such as fundraisers and other awareness-raising events in support of the agency's mission.

Young people want to get involved. It is the agency's job to get them on board with a powerful message so they will volunteer for you rather than opting to volunteer for another organization.

This volunteerism can start while they are still in high school, where students are encouraged to donate their time to a cause of interest to them and work on projects to support that effort. While in college their time is limited; however, after graduation there is ample opportunity to get them and their employers involved in your agency.

These young board members will bring their volunteer experiences back to their families, friends, and cohorts who might also be interested and join them on their next volunteer trip. Then the companies that they work for might also contribute funding or support in some other fashion.

As the recent move of the Major League Baseball All-Star Game out of Georgia in response to new Jim Crow–type election laws shows, the business community is finally stepping up and speaking out on social issues that affect their players as well as the millions of fans who attend their games. Many large corporations have funds set aside for social responsibility issues that interest them.

# CHAPTER SIXTEEN

# The Passion, the Purpose, and the Payoff

*When in the course of human events ...*
**–THOMAS JEFFERSON**

I had early success volunteering with young men sixteen to twenty-four years of age who were incarcerated on Rikers Island. This happened because the guys bought into my message that their lives were not over even though they were in jail. I further assured them that I would be there for them once they were released to help them achieve their GEDs or high school diplomas and college, followed by full employment that would result in careers.

My passion for that mission led me to create Getting Out and Staying Out, whose purpose was going to be to reduce recidivism with the payoff of careers that could lead to economic independence.

You just read my story of the past sixteen years of my life, since I moved from the corporate world at the age of sixty-eight to the not-for-profit world. I made sure to include any facts I thought you would appreciate knowing about my journey in the hope you would find similarities to your experiences that would lead you to seriously consider the nonprofit world as an encore career.

Thinking back to my very first days on Rikers Island, I am reminded of the remarkable changes that have taken place in the young men who have taken advantage of our program since it was launched in 2005. When I first met these men, they did not have high opinions of themselves, and it was very apparent. Considering where they had come from—the most challenging and problematic neighborhoods—that was not surprising.

I had no idea how smart and talented most of them were until we started to give them opportunities to express themselves, both in writing and performing while they were still on Rikers Island as well as when they were released and came to our offices for services.

I think back to our annual holiday parties when the guys presented skits and artwork that they had produced. At every year-end party, each one of them was presented with a superlative award, such as Most Improved in School, Most Eloquent Presenter, Funniest, Best Athlete, etc. Upon receiving their awards, their fellow participants and staff members would emit rousing cheers, filling the room with joy.

If a stranger had walked into any of those parties, there is no way they would have thought that any one of our guys had ever had a run-in with the law. The feelings of satisfaction, joy, fulfillment, and rebirth that I felt after every one of those parties, knowing that I had something major to do with the guys' progress, far exceeded any such feelings that I had ever had in my corporate career.

I retired from Getting Out and Staying Out (GOSO) in December of 2019 to become founder and CEO emeritus. Three months prior to that, the board of directors conducted an intensive search to find my successor. They found the right person in Dr. Jocelynne Rainey. The true success of any organization is whether the replacement of its founder can lead it to even greater successes once that person has retired, and Dr. Rainey is doing just that at GOSO.

Since I retired from GOSO, I have had time to reflect on my decision to make that drastic move sixteen years ago. I then decided to share my story with the managing editor of a prominent business leadership periodical and asked him for feedback regarding what leadership techniques he thought I had used, from a pure business point of view, to achieve my success. He said that in addition to my having achieved success transforming the lives of over ten thousand young men ages sixteen to twenty-four involved in that criminal justice system, I'd also applied transferable skills for transformational leadership.

**My question to you is: Are you that kind of visionary? Have you found a problem in our society that requires a solution that you feel you can conquer, or one you can determine with proper research?**

Many of the skills and abilities that made me a success in business were transferable and served me well in the not-for-profit world when I became a social entrepreneur and started Getting Out and Staying Out. While at GOSO, I had discussed lessons learned which have applicability for people in today's workforce. These people may be considering career pivots or encore careers, contemplating retirement, or simply downsizing due to the pandemic.

There was never any question from the day I founded GOSO that I was a leader who led by example, as well as a visionary who had recognized the social need and created an organization to fill that need.

My question to you is: Are you also that kind of visionary? Have you found a problem in our society that requires a solution that you feel you can conquer, or one you can determine with proper research?

Our society at large remains in great need of solutions for issues that continue to plague our country. Whether it is poverty in the inner city or elsewhere, Black Lives Matter, the rights of women and children, the criminal justice system, special education, job training, mental health, gun control, or one of the many others out there needing assistance, there are many opportunities available.

Most likely you have already determined that you have the leadership skills, learned during your years of for-profit experience that might be transferred to the nonprofit sector. Those skills will be tested dearly as you build a staff around you to assist in fulfilling your mission. It will take a strong team effort, without which you will have little chance of success.

Being the spokesperson for your mission is critical to your success. You will be hiring public relations consultants as well as lobbyists, but in the end, all that they can do is create opportunities for you to speak passionately on behalf of your agency. You will be the trusted face that everyone sees.

Once given those opportunities, it will be your responsibility to take advantage of those meetings to convince your potential investors as well as foundations and city and state representatives that you have a solution to a social issue that needs to be resolved, in the hope that they will support your efforts.

Nothing separates the for-profit world from the nonprofit world more than the power of networking. In the corporate for-profit world, I created a business plan and just followed it. I did little to no networking outside of working together on government affairs that affected competitors in the same industry. In the nonprofit world, I would not have succeeded without networking from the day that I started GOSO until the day that I retired.

What a social entrepreneur must do is analyze the world that he or she is planning to enter and determine what major influencers might affect his chance for success. That search will be different for every nonprofit.

Having decided to work with young men in the criminal justice system, I knew for sure that the DOC would be the primary influencer on my work, so that was where I went first. From day one, GOSO had unlimited access, within reason, on Rikers Island and in the upstate prisons. We achieved that status by following their rules and working within the system. We were guests in their house, and we would be respectful of all their rules and regulations for visiting.

Next came the Department of Education (DOE), because I needed access to the alternative high school on Rikers Island, and I wanted them to select GOSO as an alternative high school location in my offices in New York City, which was what they did.

The Mayor's Office of Criminal Justice was next on my agenda, and I quickly formed a relationship with them that allowed me to get funding for GOSO. We were also selected to form an antigun violence unit in East Harlem that we named Save East Harlem. Since we opened, we have already expanded our original footprint to an additional location in East Harlem. Because this is neighborhood work, there has to be an office within any potential site for violent occurrences, since travel between neighborhoods is dangerous due to gang presences.

This was another good example of an entrepreneur's mind at work. I could have very easily said no to the mayor's office when they asked me if I would be interested in starting an antiviolence unit separate from GOSO. However, I recognized the need for such an organization in East Harlem, since violence was on the rise all over the city.

This would require me to seek and hire brand-new staff who would have entirely different qualifications and backgrounds from the staff that presently ran GOSO. They had to be from the neighborhood. Some had been formerly incarcerated themselves. They had to understand gang culture, life in the projects, and have a network that would allow them to both anticipate potential violent events and then reach out in a timely fashion once they occurred.

When I think back to all of the logistical, political, and everyday unique situations that could have stopped me from creating Getting Out and Staying Out, I continue to be amazed that it all came to fruition. The criminal justice system has its own complicated set of quirks; however, I am quite sure that any endeavor that you might undertake will have its own set of problems that only a driven entrepreneur will be able to overcome. Your road will not always be paved by onlookers who want you to succeed, as they may have their own agendas.

Before closing, I must reemphasize the importance of your passion for your mission. You must be involved right down to the firsthand knowledge of your clients. They must know who you are. It is not like corporate leadership, where you are far removed from your customers.

Over the years I was honored with several awards, starting with the Purpose Prize that earned the agency $100,000 due to my having a successful encore career after years in the corporate world. In addition, GOSO received the Mutual of America Community Partnership Award, and I received the Manhattan Institute's Social Entrepreneur of the Year award. All the awards not only brought financial support to GOSO but they also dramatically raised awareness of a new, fledgling reentry

**Scan for Purpose Prize video**

organization that needed and received government support from both New York City and New York State.

On the federal level, I was asked to testify at the White House to help convince President Trump to sign the First Step Act. He was so impressed by the outcomes of GOSO, specifically our reducing recidivism from over 60 percent to under 15 percent, that he supported the bill to shorten mandatory minimums for nonviolent drug offenses and lessen prison terms for violators of three-strike statutes. It was one of the few bipartisan bills that he signed during his four-year term.

I wanted to be part of liberals and conservatives, Republicans, Democrats, and Independents working together for the common good. A quote from Frederick Douglass expresses my point of view on this issue:

"I would unite with anybody to do right and with nobody to do wrong."

In my opinion, bipartisanship has always been the right answer to solving the problems of our country. Hopefully the upcoming infrastructure plan, which includes some criminal justice reform, will be supported and passed by both Republicans and Democrats and become law.

When I tell people that it costs close to $350,000 to house an inmate on Rikers Island for a year, and GOSO's annual total costs to fully support every young man is only $10,000 a year, I get their attention.

As the spokesperson for GOSO, I was and still am always available to the press to speak on behalf of criminal justice reform efforts all across the United States that have made tremendous strides during my tenure at GOSO; but there are still miles to go, starting with bail reform, which might be my next area of concentration.

In the full sixteen years that I went to Rikers Island every week, working with close to ten thousand young men, not one single young man bailed out. That should tell you something—we have a bail system in this country that is reserved just for the privileged.

*MG*